NEIGHBORLINESS

NEIGHBORLINESS

FINDING THE BEAUTY OF GOD
ACROSS DIVIDING LINES

DAVID DOCUSEN

Fedd Books
P.O. Box 341973
Austin, TX 78734
www.thefeddagency.com

Published in association with The Fedd Agency, Inc., a literary agency.

ISBN: 978-1-949784-47-3
eISBN: 978-1-949784-48-0
Library of Congress Control Number: 2020910373

Some names and identifying details have been changed to protect the privacy of individuals.

Cover Design: Allison East
Cover Image: © iStock Photo

Printed in the United States of America

First Edition 20 21 22 23 / 5 4 3 2 1

For Dara, Max, Mary, Jack, and Benjamin.
We choose Jesus and share His love with others.
I love you forever.

Contents

Foreword

by Mark Batterson

The greatest commandment to love God and love your neighbor has been talked about and used so many times in sermons that sometimes it goes in one ear and out the other. It's like when you say a word too many times and it leaks a little bit of meaning. That's when you need to rediscover its meaning or introduce a new word.

Enter *Neighborliness*!

Jesus' command was not a suggestion. If He called it the great commandment, maybe we should try to be great at it. To love God fully and to love your neighbor wholeheartedly is a worldview and a lifestyle. It's the lens through which we see life. *Neighborliness* will help you apply that lens to every area of your life, as well as identify some of the blind spots you may have when it comes to loving and caring for people who are different than you.

David Docusen is one of the most approachable people I've ever met. And this book truly is an extension of who he is. In *Neighborliness*, he takes some of the most difficult subjects to talk about—racial conflict and economic disparities among them—and makes them approachable. He infuses these discussions with much-needed grace. David takes the message of Jesus and he shows you and me what it looks like to walk in and live out that message, not just in church or with a small group of friends, but in the discordant realities present in America.

David's vision for the church and the nation is beautiful and contagious. He brings hope and light to conversations that often feel daunting and dark. And he is not pretending that he hasn't made any mistakes. That's how all of us learn! He openly shares some of his fumbles and struggles, which makes this book all the better! I've been honored to walk alongside him as he learns more about these issues, cultivates conversations based on what he learns, and enacts lasting change in his community. I have learned so much from him, including the attitude with which to approach these topics.

We are often so afraid of making mistakes or saying the wrong thing, especially in conversations regarding social justice and racial unity, that we just freeze—too afraid to speak or act. In *Neighborliness*, David clearly displays through personal stories and wisdom from activists and theologians that we cannot let fear of mistakes keep us from kingdom work.

The dividing lines in America are not representative of God's heart for His people. We are to be ambassadors for truth, justice, unity, peace, and diversity. After all, Jesus Himself was the embodiment of these ideals. He crossed dividing lines, challenged the status quo, and consistently interacted with people who were different from Him. He spoke truth when it was difficult; He became enraged at injustice and sought for a more just society; He brought unity through amplifying the voices of the marginalized and empowering the young and overlooked; He extended peace to everyone He met; and He came to the world to extend salvation to all people, no exceptions.

That being said, this book will change your perspective, your family, and your community. If you are ready to be an ambassador for unity, keep reading.

—Mark Batterson
NYT bestselling author of Circle Maker

Opening Prayer:
The Lord's Prayer

Our Father, who art in heaven,

hallowed be your name.

May your kingdom come,

and your will be done,

on earth as in heaven.

Give us today our daily bread.

Forgive us our sins

as we forgive those who sin against us.

Lead us not into temptation,

but deliver us from evil;

for yours are the kingdom

and the power and the glory

forever and ever. Amen.[1]

INTRODUCTION

The Day I Opened My Eyes

We all look alike, I thought to myself. My heart raced as I looked across the room.

Standing behind a simple metal podium in an elementary school auditorium, I was about to preach as I had done each Sunday for the previous five years. Standing in front of my congregation who had become family to me, I was not prepared for my heart to be broken.

Tears filled my eyes, and I was rendered speechless.

I am not sure why it happened on this day, but I finally saw that our beautiful expression of faith at Center City Church only included people who looked just like me. I didn't know how we got to this point.

***

Center City Church started in my home on August 19, 2009 with seventeen people who were committed to a simple expression of faith. I looked at my living room congregation that night and said, "If this is real, it will spread."

We embarked on a raw and beautiful journey. We spread the news of a new church in the community through word-of-mouth invitations to our home for dinner. We started meeting around our dining room table and then spilled into our living room as the numbers slowly grew each week. My earliest memories of starting this church are closely tied to store-brand pasta and my wife Dara's homemade marinara sauce.

Over the next few years, our church family grew from seventeen people gathered in my living room to around 200 people meeting at Elizabeth Traditional Elementary School's auditorium. It was simple and beautiful. Natural light flooded the room from the windows along the left side of the auditorium, and we could see the Uptown Charlotte skyline out of those windows while we worshiped. Located one mile southeast of the center of the city, Elizabeth is a walkable neighborhood filled with boutique stores, local coffee shops, and bakeries. Mature trees form canopies over the streets of century-old homes that have been renovated while still keeping their historic charm.

The group of friends God brought to us changed my family; they taught us to express our faith in a way that I had only ever hoped could be true. We experienced unreasonable generosity, care, joy, and compassion. Center City Church became a tangible reality of my long-held belief that people long to be known and know others. We had finally found a place where we could experience a sense of belonging and community.

***

I stared at the podium for several moments with tears in my eyes.

Our word-of-mouth approach was genuine and seemed to be working. We were growing because people were inviting their friends. Church growth experts say that word of mouth is the most effective form of advertising, and we were constantly growing by a few people each week. Our team had a running joke that we were experiencing the slowest explosion of growth in the history of the church. We didn't care about any of that though. We simply enjoyed each other and the new friends that consistently expanded our circles of friendship.

In my speechlessness that particular Sunday morning, the congregation looked back at me and probably figured I was just having a moment with the Holy Spirit. They patiently waited as I tried to formulate my thoughts. But as I looked back at them, I was finally *feeling* the reality that most of our friends were young and white.

"Everyone looks alike."

The walls of our beautiful church crashed around me on the Sunday that God opened my eyes. We were a tight-knit community of twenty and thirty-somethings living and working in Uptown Charlotte. Our church was 95 percent middle class and white.

And the plaid. There was so much plaid.

I have no idea how long I stared at our church family that morning. I finally looked down through my blurry, tear-filled eyes and proceeded to preach the most scatter-brained and incoherent message of my ministry career. I laughed it off with our associate pastor, Joseph, after the service, "Can't win 'em all, right?"

After service, I remember writing down a phrase in my journal, "Like people invite like people." My confessions continued as I cried over my journal, "Our beautiful church looks nothing like our beautiful city." The day I opened my eyes, I started a journey that would deeply impact my relationship with God and with others.

***

I never thought of myself as a pastor that shied away from hard topics. However, I was becoming increasingly aware that my silence on the topic of racial and economic inequality was directly related to my lack of knowledge, understanding, and curiosity. I was silent on these topics because I did not have words readily available to articulate or contribute anything substantive to the conversation.

In his TED talk "The Danger of Silence," author, professor, and poet Clint Smith talks about engaging people across dividing lines. In the video, he encourages people to speak up against ignorance and injustice. Clint said, "Explore the silence of your own life. Fill those spaces. Name them and share them."[2]

In hindsight, my silence spoke louder than I realized.

My circle of friends didn't include people of color because my entire worldview from birth was white, middle class, and blind to the realities of my fellow classmates and peers. I didn't know what I didn't know. And I spent no extra effort exploring how race and economics in our country impacts my neighbors.

In high school, I could sense the way black and brown students at Lake Brantley High School were treated with less respect by white students. I heard the off-color jokes from my white friends about students of color. I didn't like those jokes, but I still chuckled to make sure I properly fit into social circles. I was not telling the jokes, but my silence spoke louder than I realized.

Can you relate to this silence in your life? Have you participated in conversations with people in your relational circle that have devolved into disparaging conversations about people unlike you? How do you respond?

Dr. Martin Luther King Jr. said, "In the end we will not remember the words of our enemies, but the silence of our friends." Understanding the danger of silence leads to using our voices to love our neighbors.

***

Imagine the heartbreak I experienced after realizing that we had spent five years of our lives cultivating a beautiful community, only to realize that our version of beauty did not include the diversity that drew Dara and me to Charlotte in the first place.

I found myself in moments of brokenness and repentance asking God to open my eyes to my own blindness that kept me from seeing such a lack of cultural diversity. I reached out to several pastors across Charlotte that had a beautiful expression of diversity in their congregations. I spent countless hours listening, learning, and asking questions. Pastor Kelvin was one of those gracious pastors that spent time mentoring me. He challenged me to look inward before addressing issues among our church family.

I had always been amazed at the diversity in his church. I was growing increasingly more curious as to how it happened. Kelvin is a white man in his early fifties with a rich southern accent that sounds like it has been marinating in a bottle of Tennessee bourbon. He is southern through and through. However, his church felt like a meeting of the United Nations. Upon arriving at the church, the lobby greets you with flags from over sixty countries. Each flag is a representation of the nationality of people that attend his church. Thousands of worshipers gather each weekend to sing together and engage in learning from Pastor Kelvin's teaching. Every time I see worship represented in the book of Revelation, I see diversity, and I can't help but think that worshiping in a multicultural setting is a foretaste of heaven on earth.

"David," Pastor Kelvin said slowly and patiently, "How many black friends do you have?"

He leaned back in his chair and smiled as I squirmed. I talked about people of color that had been in and out of our church. I talked about my friend Chris. He was the only black friend that I consistently hung out with in my predominantly white group of friends.

Kelvin leaned across the table with a gentle smile and warm tone in his voice and cut to the core of my being. "I'm not asking you how many people of color you know; I'm asking how many are genuinely your friends? Who is comfortable enough to open up to you? How many friends trust you enough to tell you their experience of what it means to be a person of color in our country?"

I was stumped, ashamed, and embarrassed. I realized I had never had *that* conversation with any of my non-white friends.

"Start with prayer," he said, "and ask God to open your heart to listen to and learn from a new group of friends. I'm here for you if you need anything. God will bring you the right people along your path as long as you are ready to make new friends."

Soon after I started to pray about these things I was wrestling with, I was invited to a prayer meeting that forever changed my life.

***

I arrived a few minutes late to a small gathering of friends praying in the lobby of an old warehouse that was renovated into a church in West Charlotte. Four metal-framed chairs were positioned in an imperfect circle. Two white men and two black men were taking turns praying out loud for the neighborhoods surrounding this church. When one person would pray, the other three would sincerely agree in those prayers. I was struck by their sincerity.

A few weeks prior, a friend invited me to join this intimate gathering. I was new to the neighborhood and, if I'm honest, I was still nervous about being the new guy and fitting into established circles of relationships. I finally got over myself and joined to pray.

These four friends had been gathering together for the

past several months. Violent crime, drug-addiction, gang activity, failing schools, and families living in poverty were pervasive in their community.

"God, I've had enough of the pain. I'm asking you to send your healing power to this community." Pastor Ken prayed with authority, "Please send us more workers because you have said the harvest is plentiful, but the workers are few. It won't come from the government. It won't come from a new nonprofit. It won't come from the businesses that continue to move into our neighborhood. It will come from your church. Your healing power will flow through your church."

I felt welcome before I even met the people with whom I was praying that day. My spirit resonated as if I had been a part of the family all along. We prayed like we meant it until 1:00 p.m. When the meeting ended, Pastor Ken looked at me with genuine love in his eyes. "Brother, you are welcome here." He hugged me. I fought back tears as he said, "You are welcome in our community, and I'm here to serve you however I can."

I was blown away by the power of his hospitality.

Over the next several months, God blessed me with an increasing number of friendships in West Charlotte. The Wednesday prayer group slowly grew each week. My new friends joined me in prayer as I was navigating an opportunity to move Center City Church from the affluent Elizabeth community to a unique location at the corner of Freedom Drive and Berryhill Avenue.

1

The Other Half of the Greatest Commandment

The religion of Jesus makes the love-ethic central.
—Howard Thurman, *Jesus and the Disinherited*

What do you think of when you hear the word *neighbor*?

Maybe you think of Mr. Rogers singing as he puts on his red cardigan. Maybe you think of covering your ears with your pillow as your neighbor blasts music on a Tuesday night. (*Who parties on a Tuesday night?*) Maybe you think of your childhood when you would visit the old man who lived down the street from you who smelled like cigars. Maybe you think of your lifelong best friend.

Neighbor is a vast, expansive term that holds different connotations, experiences, and memories for everyone. When I think of the word *neighbor*, I think of a certain conversation between Jesus and a lawyer.

Jesus attracted large crowds throughout His public ministry. Word spread quickly throughout the community as He was healing blind people, casting out demons, and speaking openly against powerful political figures.

One day, like many other days, a crowd swelled in a public square as Jesus was engaged in a fast-paced and brilliant debate about religious matters of the day. The scene was set for a public theological showdown.

The religious leaders viewed Jesus as a threat to their positions of power within the community. They consistently attempted to trap Jesus into saying something that would lead to His arrest. As we find out later in the gospel accounts, they stopped at nothing to silence His voice.

"Of all the commandments," a man asked Jesus, "which is the most important?"

The person asking the question was an expert in religious law. A lawyer. A teacher of religion. This is significant because the community gathered around a dizzying number of religious laws that set the tone for the culture—law was life. As an expert in religious law, this lawyer would have been widely respected and given special favor economically, politically, and socially. His eyes were fixed on Jesus in anticipation as his question hung in the air.

There were over six hundred commandments to consider.

Without missing a beat, Jesus answers the question with striking simplicity: "Love the Lord your God with all your heart, all your soul, all your mind, and all your strength." However, He did not stop there. Unprovoked and unprompted, He continued, "The second is this: 'Love your neighbor as yourself.' There is no commandment greater than these" (Mark 12:30–31).

Jesus simply and clearly gave us the answer to a really

important question. Stated differently, we could say, "What is the most important thing we should focus on when we are exploring matters of faith?" His answer is to love God and neighbors. This simple phrase sums up six hundred commands. It seems as though we should pay more attention to this passage. After all, Jesus said it's more important than everything else.

WHO IS MY NEIGHBOR?

"Who is my neighbor?"

I posed this question to a small group that was studying Mark 12:28–34 on a Tuesday evening in Detroit, Michigan.

"In my opinion," Scott replied, "my neighbor is the person who lives next door to me in my neighborhood."

I responded, "You live in a gated neighborhood in the suburbs. What about folks that attend church with you that live in some of the high-poverty communities around Detroit?"

"They can be my friends," Scott replied matter-of-factly, "but they are not my neighbors."

I looked across the room, noticing Kendra grip her pen a bit tighter. My heart began to race as I realized that Scott unknowingly delivered an unexpected blow to Kendra. She was a resident of one of the high-poverty communities that I mentioned.

"If I'm not your neighbor, Scott," she said strongly, "then what am I doing here?"

Moments like this have happened in churches countless times. Unsuspecting white people make comments that they do not realize will hurt or bring pain to people of color. All too often, these type of conversations in churches lead to further division because people have not been educated on matters related to race and economics. Most middle- and upper-class white people grew up learning a version of history that was written by someone in the dominant group. That means they learned American and world history as predominantly white history.

Education may have led us to this point, but education can also lead us into a more God-honoring understanding of our past so that we can start finding a new path forward. Opening our eyes to see how our silence and ignorance affects people who are different than we are is the first step. Then we have to figure out how to cross the street and begin a conversation. Our neighbors aren't dependent on our zip code; our neighbors are all around us. Whether we ignore them and turn them away or welcome them as friends is up to us.

***

Neighborliness is the behavior of Christians who seek to embody the love, understanding, curiosity, kindness, and care of Jesus. His life showed us how to love others with open arms. Jesus was constantly crossing the street and beginning conversations with people that were different from Him.

He calls us to do the same. When we look at Jesus' lifestyle, we can immediately see that He didn't just hang out with people who looked and lived like Him.

- Jesus encouraged a rich man to pursue spiritual riches over earthly wealth (Mark 10:17–31).
- Jesus prophesied to a Samaritan woman—Jews did not associate with Samaritans (John 4:1–26).
- Jesus loved children and celebrated their innocence (Matthew 18:1–5).
- Jesus recognized and healed a blind beggar named Bartimaeus (Mark 10:46–52).
- Jesus patiently welcomed a skeptic named Thomas (John 20:24–29).
- Jesus highlighted the generosity of a poor widow (Luke 21:1–4).
- Jesus forgave a convicted criminal and welcomed him into the family of God (Luke 23:39–43).
- Jesus spent extravagant amounts of time with sinners like you and me (Matthew, Mark, Luke, and John).

When Jesus said, "Love your neighbor," He wasn't talking about the people who lived right next to Him in Galilee. Acts 1:8 paints a vivid picture of the diverse family of God. As He is preparing to physically leave the earth, Jesus promises the presence of the Holy Spirit to remain and empower everyone who believes in Him. He said, "You will receive power when the Holy Spirit comes upon you. And you will be my witnesses, telling people about me everywhere—in Jerusalem, throughout Judea, in Samaria, and to the ends of the earth."

His ministry, His reach, and His friendship expanded far past Galilee Drive. So, too, should ours.

HOW DO I LOVE MY NEIGHBOR?

The lawyer wanted something quantifiable to achieve success. But here Jesus shows that following God is not a checklist or a moral scale for weighing good and bad deeds. Many of the 600 laws dealt with possessions and behavior. But through His answer, Jesus shows that following God is first and foremost about love and relationship.

The Bible tells us to love in truth and action. So when it comes to loving our neighbor, what does it look like in a practical way? Loving our neighbor looks like seeing her the way that God sees her. Loving our neighbor means intentionally getting to know him and learning about his experiences. Loving our neighbor includes educating ourselves on issues that are important to our brothers and sisters in Christ.

You may look at those who are different from you and say, "We have absolutely nothing in common." While many friendships include differing backgrounds and experiences, there are similarities that every person shares. We are all:

- Made in the image of God (Genesis 1:27)
- Worthy of love and belonging (1 John 3:1)
- Made for a purpose and plan established by God (Jeremiah 29:11)

These are the things that connect us. When you see someone who looks and lives differently than you and you think it would be impossible to connect with them, remember these inherent and irrefutable truths. Recognize your shared humanity. And remember to be curious.

"Max," I recently told my oldest son, "The thing people can most easily talk about is themselves. That's not a bad thing. You should never be in a setting where a conversation is going nowhere because you can always ask someone to describe the place that they were born, their favorite vacation, or something fun that's recently happened in their life." Learning to build relationships across dividing lines includes asking intentional questions about people and their experiences. Relationships are built through sharing the journey of life together. We see this in our relationship with God. Knowing and being known by God produces an unimaginable depth of love.

I have learned that if I long to honor the call to love my neighbor as myself, I need to get to know more people who are created in the image of God that don't look like or come from the same economic upbringing as me. Getting to know people from different backgrounds is not always easy, however. Patience is a key ingredient. I have resolved to hold my tongue a lot more when I am offended. This discipline allows me to patiently wait for my emotions to subside. I cannot think of a single time in my life when I regretted waiting for my emotions to settle before responding to someone with whom I disagreed on a certain topic. I can, however, think of plenty of times when I have spoken too quickly and said something I could not take back.

Instead of reacting in anger when I feel defensive, I can ask better questions to learn where the pain is coming from in the life of my friend. I have to be humble and realize that I do not understand everyone else's perspectives, and I need to take the time to listen and learn from others.

Additionally, I have been challenged to do as much of the work as I can on my own. I can accomplish this by reading books on topics of racial and economic division in the church and in our culture as a whole. There are so many books that have deeply impacted me and led me to greater understanding of racial and economic matters from a Christ-centered perspective—books such as *The Color of Compromise: The Truth About the American Church's Complicity in Racism* by Jamar Tisby and *Rich Christians in an Age of Hunger: Moving from Affluence to Generosity* by Ronald Sider. I have included a larger list in the recommended reading section on page 206.

We cannot expect friends from different backgrounds to teach us everything about their experience. That expectation is exhausting and it does not honor your friends. We have the ability to learn without asking them to relive painful experiences every time we are ready to learn. Simply stated, we need to choose to learn on our own. If we have an informed perspective of the history and experience of our neighbors, we will find that they may be more willing to have a substantive conversation. We cannot expect our friends to be our sole educators.

We love our neighbor when we recognize our commonalities, become curious about her experiences, and learn about the things she is passionate about. We love our neighbor when we no longer think of our differences as an obstacle, but rather as an illuminating light.

THE BEST EXPRESSION OF FAITH

The response Jesus gave to the lawyer used to bother me. If I cannot answer that my favorite ice cream is butter pecan *and* rocky road, it doesn't seem fair that Jesus could give two answers to such an important question.

However, the brilliance of the answer Jesus gave is found in the fact that a person cannot truly love God with all of his or her heart, soul, mind, and strength without also expressing love to his or her neighbors. Loving God and loving neighbors are to be understood as distinct actions that can be fully expressed in tandem. Biblical scholar Nancy Duff explained, "The two commandments cannot be understood as interchangeable, but neither are they severed."[3]

Love toward God is not intended to occur in isolation; love toward God naturally results in love for our neighbors as well. The more that I explore this passage, the more I realize I need to allow the Holy Spirit to lead and guide me in this simple command every day. Here are some questions that I have begun asking myself as I allow the Holy Spirit to examine my life and point out anything that doesn't match the spirit of neighborliness that Jesus calls me to embody.

- When was the last time I patiently listened to someone from a very different background from mine?
- Do my friendships reflect the diversity of the city in which I am living?

- Do I have any friends from another race or economic situation who will honestly talk to me about their experiences? If so, when was the last time I had that conversation?
- Do I listen and seek to understand when I am challenged by someone else's perspectives on matters of race and economics, or am I defensive and holding tight to my own views?

David prayed in Psalm 139:23–24, "Search me, O God, and know my heart; test me and know my anxious thoughts. Point out anything in me that offends you, and lead me along the path of everlasting life." In order to make an impact in our churches and communities, we must humble ourselves, question our motives, and allow God to search our hearts for any lingering prejudice or pride.

As the body of Christ, we have given quite a bit of attention to the first half of the greatest commandment. Let's give proper attention to the other half of the greatest commandment. Is your pursuit of knowing, loving, and understanding your neighbors as important to you as loving God? True passion for God will naturally lead to loving others regardless of their racial or economic background. If a natural outflow of our faith is a homogeneous circle of friends, we are missing a key component in the life of faith.

Race and economics have divided our communities and churches for far too long.

The gospel compels us to learn how to explore matters of race, economics, and friendship with grace and patience. If we are going to experience life-giving and God-honoring relationships across dividing lines in our lives, we must look inward first. The hard work of self-examination flows naturally from hearts that are pursuing the call to neighborliness that Jesus included as most important in our expression of faith.

2

The Tale of Two Cities

Living the gospel means desiring for your neighbor and
your neighbor's family that which you desire for yourself
and your family.
—**John Perkins,** *Restoring At-Risk Communities*

I could see Berryhill Avenue from the window in my office
at the new location of Center City Church. Ever since our
church family made the four-mile move from Elizabeth to
West Charlotte, this view served as a constant reminder of
the visceral division in our community.

On the left side of Berryhill is the Bryant Park neighborhood. Beautiful single-family homes and townhomes
range from $350,000–$500,000. On the right side of Berryhill is the historic Camp Greene neighborhood. Weathered
homes that have withstood generations of poverty fill Camp
Greene. Bryant Park is a predominantly white community.
Camp Greene is a predominantly black community.

A joint study between Harvard University and University of California, Berkeley highlighted a devastating reality

in my hometown of Charlotte, North Carolina. A child born into poverty has a 4 percent chance of escaping the cycle of generational poverty and reaching the upper levels of economic income. Let that one sink in for a moment. In my hometown, 96 percent of kids born into poverty will never have the same opportunities as other kids to reach higher levels of income.[4]

The Harvard/UC Berkeley study began referring to Charlotte as "The Tale of Two Cities" because of the wide gap between the opportunities provided for kids born into higher levels of income and kids born into poverty. Nowhere is this more evident than one mile west of the heart of the city on Berryhill Avenue.

A row of perfectly manicured townhomes on Berryhill Avenue directly face the front porches of a few homes in Camp Greene. I regularly drive down Berryhill and pray for my neighbors. I pray that God would give them courage to cross the street. I ask God to teach us, as a community, how to move past perceived differences and find friendship across culturally dividing lines. However, all too often, my neighbors are separated by a two-lane road and a world of opportunities.

***

Andrea moved into the Bryant Park community in 2015.

When advertisements for a new neighborhood close to the city caught her attention, she decided to explore the option further. The one-mile commute to her office in Uptown Charlotte cut thirty minutes off of her stop-and-go commute from the North Charlotte suburbs.

Bryant Park was a brand-new neighborhood that was right on the edge of the affluent neighborhoods adjacent to the city. The proximity to Uptown was appealing and the prices seemed right for her family to move into a new three bedroom home. After weighing out all of the options, she decided to move forward with the purchase. Andrea closed on the home in August of 2015, just in time to enjoy a few weeks of summer vacation with her husband and two kids as they settled into their new neighborhood.

The first sign that something was off in the neighborhood came when she got a notification on her cell phone from the NextDoor neighborhood app. "ALERT," the community posting read in all caps, "Two black boys riding their bikes through Bryant Park wearing hoodies. Be aware."

Andrea was stunned.

"I can't believe people still talk like this," she said to her husband, John.

"Don't let it get to you, love. I'm sure it's just a weird neighbor. Every neighborhood's got one."

Andrea was bothered, but she let it go.

The second sign came from another alert on the same app. "Be on the lookout," the post declared, "A black man is selling magazines door to door and he looks nervous."

Andrea was becoming concerned that this was more than one weird neighbor.

Another person had already posted a reply: "The same man came to my door and he was incredibly kind. He was sweating profusely because it's ninety-seven degrees today. I offered him a glass of ice water, and we had a great conversation. You sound like a jerk."

The author of the original post replied, "Sorry to be judgmental. I just wanted to make sure our neighborhood is safe."

Another person replied, "Why does a black man sweating in the Carolina heat while selling magazines make you feel unsafe?"

The author of the post quickly deleted the thread.

Andrea's heart was heavy when she saw similar posts from neighbors that seemed to be fearful of residents of the neighborhoods surrounding Bryant Park. She started to explore the history of her new neighborhood. Her heart sank when she realized that Bryant Park and the high-poverty community across the street—Camp Greene—used to be one neighborhood. Families that lived in Camp Greene were forced out after developers purchased and promptly tore down over two hundred homes. She did not know about this when she purchased the home. Even so, she could not shake the feeling that she had unintentionally contributed to disrupting the historic rhythm of the Camp Greene neighborhood. Without her knowledge, she had purchased a home in a neighborhood that was loaded with complex and emotional stories tied to racial and economic matters.

Neighborhood kids from Camp Greene were doing what they had done for decades: riding bikes in the street and chasing each other around as their imaginations ran wild. The neighborhood may have a new name, but their favorite hill to race down was still there. The new neighborhood now included families from a different economic class that moved into the same location that was once inhabited by friends and families of these boys.

Andrea couldn't get the phrase "Love your neighbor as yourself" out of her head. She opened her Bible to Mark 12:28–34. Jesus engaged with people who were different from Him; with people who came from different backgrounds, believed different things, and lived differently than Him. She noticed that Jesus intentionally talked with people across ethnic, religious, economic, gender, and generational lines. He was judged harshly for these actions, yet He continued to reach across culturally dividing lines to know and enjoy His neighbors. Andrea knew that if Bryant Park was ever going to feel like home, she was going to have to learn more about what it meant to be friends with her neighbors across Berryhill Avenue in Camp Greene.

Andrea was taking her first step inward toward modeling neighborliness for her community. She knew that if her neighborhood was ever going to change, she needed to change first.

"Kids, get your shoes on," she announced up the stairwell toward the bedrooms. "We're going on a walk."

They had started a habit of taking a family walk before dinner a few nights a week. Instead of confining their walk to their neighborhood of similar style homes that evening in Bryant Park, they chose to cross Berryhill Avenue to walk the streets of Camp Greene.

"John, there is no better way for us to get to know our neighbors than to physically get out of our house and make ourselves available," she said while tying her son's shoes.

"We need to meet our neighbors. And not just the ones that live directly around us. Let's walk."

***

Jasmine and Jamila have been friends for thirty years. They grew up four houses away from each other in the Camp Greene neighborhood and both still live in the same community one mile west of Uptown Charlotte.

Jasmine has three elementary-aged kids and a job working the first shift at the Amazon factory in West Charlotte. Jamila has two preschool kids and works second shift at a diner in the city. They organize their work schedules so that they can care for each other's children while the other is at work.

The kids were playing in the front yard on a crisp October afternoon in Camp Greene. Jasmine invited Jamila over to have a drink on the porch. The neighborhood was quiet. The kids' laughter echoed off the large pine trees that towered over the homes.

Jasmine's mind was racing.

"I never said that I didn't want nice things in our neighborhood," Jasmine said as she swayed casually on the porch swing. "I'm all for a new grocery store and retail shops within walking distance of our house."

"Same here," Jamila responded. "I heard about some new restaurants that are coming into the neighborhood. That sounds good to me."

Jasmine had just read that Camp Greene had been listed as one of the top ten communities for investment by various local real estate agencies.

"I'm all for upgrades in our neighborhood. I just want to be able to stay after the new things arrive," Jasmine said as she stared down her familiar street. She continued, "Do you remember when Grandma Sadie was forced to leave her house a few years ago? That was hard. We helped each other out a lot."

Jasmine and Jamila finished their drink and called for the kids. The sun was setting over the tree line in Camp Greene.

***

"A great developer has great instincts."

"Anticipate the growth of our city."

"Build neighborhoods in the path of future growth."

Eric could recite dozens of axioms that his father had passed down to him over the years. Eric spent the first twelve years of his real estate career learning the ropes from his father, Dan. He started off by handling much of the administrative paperwork and filings on properties his father was developing. Continuing in his father's footsteps was always a part of his plan. He loved the entire process of creating a new neighborhood.

Many days, Eric would drive his Ford F-150 through the unfinished streets of new neighborhoods that were being developed. He would allow his imagination to run wild as he envisioned families receiving keys to their home for the first time and children riding bikes through the streets. Neighbors that didn't even know each other would become lifelong friends because of the neighborhood he was building. He loved the fact that he was following in the family tradition of building neighborhoods in the Charlotte community.

Eric, like his father before him, enjoyed a measure of success that led to a comfortable life in the Queen City. His family purchased a home fifteen minutes from Uptown

Charlotte in a charming and well-manicured neighborhood called Myers Park. The church his family had attended since he was a boy was within walking distance of their home. The familiar streets of South Charlotte led to a satisfying life for Eric and his wife, Heather.

The instinctive feeling his father taught him to recognize was palpable when he drove through the streets of West Charlotte. Largely overlooked by developers for several decades, Eric felt that growth would naturally start to move west of the city. Single family homes could be purchased for $40,000–$60,000. Dozens of parcels of real estate were abandoned, easily identified by the plywood over the windows. Empty and overgrown lots were common. The neighborhood was less than a minute away from the western border of Uptown Charlotte.

"This is it," he thought to himself.

Eric purchased his first home in Camp Greene for $42,000 and promptly rented it back to the family that previously owned the home at $475 per month. Over the next several years, Eric assembled an investment team that would eventually purchase over two hundred homes proximate to each other on the eastern border of the historic Camp Greene neighborhood. Some families chose to move out of Camp Greene after selling their home. Many chose to rent their homes back from Eric's investment group after completing the sale.

"What is going to happen to all the families that have lived in Camp Greene once your team assembles all of the properties you are pursuing?" Heather asked as she peered over the top of the latest James Patterson thriller she was reading.

"I'm not totally sure," he replied. He could hear a subtle hint of concern in her voice. "We will make sure to give the families plenty of notice, though."

Eric had just returned from a public meeting that is required when a new neighborhood is being developed. He poured a two-finger glass of Woodford Reserve and let out a deep sigh. The meeting went as well as he could have expected. It was still stressful, though.

Forty-three people from the Camp Greene neighborhood attended the meeting to discuss plans that were recently made public to redevelop a small section of Camp Greene into a new neighborhood that would be called Bryant Park.

"What will happen to all the homes that have been here for decades?"

"Why does our neighborhood need a new name? Are you trying to rename the entire neighborhood, or just the part with the new homes?"

"What plans do you have to ensure that two-hundred families will be able to find adequate housing when you tear down this neighborhood and replace it with homes ten times as expensive as the ones that are currently here?"

"What will happen to the property taxes of the residents of Camp Greene when these new homes are built?"

This was Eric's least favorite part of the job. He knew the basic range of questions that would come, but it didn't make the evening any more enjoyable. He did not have answers to many of the questions related to where families would go. That bothered him, but his team had mutually agreed with families on a selling price for their homes. That was enough to assuage his conscience.

We are giving fair market value, he thought to himself, even if he knew the families would not be able to buy another home at that same price. Charlotte was experiencing a shortage of 34,000 units of affordable housing. The demand for housing grew each time another new neighborhood was developed in a historically high-poverty community. But he was not an economist or a nonprofit leader that dealt with families in high-poverty communities. His job was to instinctively find land that he could develop into neighborhoods for families to enjoy for generations to come. He compartmentalized his job as a developer and his role in the affordable housing crisis that was regularly highlighted in the news.

Eric enjoyed the final bit of Woodford Reserve and retired to bed for the evening. Another day of development awaited him early the next morning.

Tangible Dividing Lines

Andrea, Jasmine, Jamila, Grandma Sadie, and Eric all play significant roles in the way cities are developed. All experience the stark dividing lines in our culture that separate us and lead to misunderstandings, pain, and confusion. These scenarios play out on a regular basis in cities across the country. Gentrification is a complicated issue because it brings a tangibility to these dividing lines.

Angela bought a property that was a great investment less than a mile from Uptown Charlotte. She had no clue that her family's purchase of this home would immediately put her at odds with neighbors that had lived in her neighborhood for several decades.

Instead of letting her guilt keep her isolated in Bryant Park, she chose to view her neighborhood as those who lived within walking distance of her home. She eliminated an invisible boundary by crossing Berryhill Avenue with her family. A smile and a wave to her neighbors across the street eventually led to conversations with new friends from very different backgrounds. Genuine friendships are born when people learn to courageously cross dividing lines.

Jasmine and Jamila could instinctively feel the walls closing in on their neighborhood. The sight of white men in luxury cars driving slowly through their neighborhood became a normal occurrence. The once peaceful sounds of laughter bouncing off of the tall pine trees in their neighborhood were now accompanied by the low rumble of cement trucks and the rapid-fire bursts from nail guns.

Peter Moskowitz described what was happening around Jasmine and Jamila's neighborhood in his book *How to Kill a City: Gentrification, Inequality, and the Fight for the Neighborhood.* He said gentrification includes displacement of families that have lived in communities for generations. This leads to loss of nuance and culture of historic neighborhoods and brings an influx of wealth and whiteness into communities that had previously been inhabited by families from various racial backgrounds.[5]

After Bryant Park was developed, residents in Camp Greene began to see their property values incrementally increase and they were constantly being offered cash for their homes. Jasmine and Jamila both resisted the temptation of $80,000 cash because they knew that amount of money could not buy them another home they would desire in Charlotte. The stress of rising taxes put a burden on both of them, but they found various ways to make it work.

I have met countless people like Jasmine and Jamila. Their shared bond includes a longtime friendship and a willingness to do whatever it takes to make the financial realities of their lives work. In many ways, I am convinced that the spirit of neighborliness that Jesus calls us to in the greatest commandment is beautifully on display in historically high-poverty communities. If you have not spent time with families that live in neighborhoods like Camp Greene, you may have formed an incomplete narrative that is told of communities that are below the median area income in your city.

Jasmine and Jamila's story highlights a term I came across in my studies called *helping networks*. This is accomplished when multiple families come together to support each other in various aspects of life. A helping network in a community like Camp Greene looks like: childcare during abnormal work hours; rides to and from work, church, school, and shared grocery runs; financial assistance when needed; sharing the ups and downs of life.

The disruption of helping networks is one of the largely unseen and unrecognized traumas that accompanies gentrification. Jasmine mentions Grandma Sadie when she is talking with Jamila. Grandma Sadie has known Jasmine and Jamila for their entire lives. Retired from the Tyson Chicken factory, Sadie lives on a small but manageable pension and joyfully watches the kids when both Jasmine and Jamila are working at the same time on the same day. Grandma Sadie sold her home to Eric's investment group and rented back the property. She did not know, however, that her rental would not be long term.

Many developers will use various limited liability corporations (LLCs) under different names as they are assembling homes for a new neighborhood. By the time the neighborhood pieces together that one group is buying large numbers of homes proximate to each other in their neighborhood, it is oftentimes too late to slow the momentum of redevelopment.

Grandma Sadie is given no choice in the matter and must move when her lease is not renewed. There is nothing illegal about this type of development practice, but the ethical nature of the practice can certainly be questioned.

I also do not believe that gentrification is always a bad thing. Jackelyn Hwang, an assistant professor of sociology at Stanford University, defines gentrification as an influx of investment and the presence of middle- or upper-income residents into previously low-income neighborhoods.[6] The development of neighborhoods is not a bad thing, particularly when it brings more diversity to homogeneous communities. Research has shown that students from diverse schools demonstrate lower levels of racial fears and stereotypes.[7] Additionally, students who study in an integrated class setting consistently score at the same level or higher than predominantly white schools.[8]

Community redevelopment can be a good thing if developers work with residents, businesses, and community leaders to *add to* a community instead of strip away the history and beauty of historic communities in the name of profit. While I do believe that development can be good, I also believe that the motivation of developers will shape the destiny and destination of residents who have lived in high-poverty communities for generations. If *profit at any cost* is the only metric used to measure success, the motivation will not reflect the spirit of neighborliness. I truly believe that business practices do not have to be divorced from the expectations of generosity and joy in the Bible.

The same instinct that developers have to build a great business is the same instinct that God can use as a unique tool for justice and equity in the neighborhoods they build. Equity is accomplished when two or more racial groups are standing on relatively equal footing.[9] Holistic thinking about work and faith will lead to practices that bring healing to our communities and equal footing to all our neighbors.

Eric is not the bad guy in this story. Far from it. His business ethic is the product of the way that he was raised and mentored. This does not, however, excuse him from accountability if he genuinely desires to align his business practices with his faith. Eric has a unique opportunity to shape the city he loves. The spirit of neighborliness would require him to think through the way his actions holistically help or harm his neighbors.

The residents of Camp Greene called the neighborhood Eric redeveloped their home. If his literal brother or sister lived in Camp Greene, how would his motivation change toward the way that he pursued the accumulation of the land and the redevelopment of the neighborhood? When he thought about how his role in redevelopment affected the affordable housing crisis, Eric had *cognitive dissonance*, the mental discomfort experienced after taking actions that appear to be in conflict with our starting preferences.[10] We have cognitive dissonance in our faith when we disassociate our behavior in business from our faith. Eric's recalibration can include exploring what the community can look like when developers and longtime residents come together with a shared imagination. Eric's story is played out in various ways across vocational endeavors.

If your story is similar to Eric's, I would ask you to consider taking some time to question how your business practices line up with the call to love God and neighbors—all of your neighbors. Are you conducting your life in a way that your vocation reflects the spirit of neighborliness? Have you settled into unhealthy patterns that disassociate your vocational goals from the faith that informs the rest of your life? Could you enjoy a meal with the people who your vocational efforts impact with a clear heart and a clean conscience?

The spirit of neighborliness calls us to look holistically at our lives and the result of our actions and behaviors. Bob Goff, one of the most joyful people I've ever met, challenges you and me to take the first step toward embodying neighborliness by asking the question: "How is your faith working for everyone around you?"[11]

Before God can use your business, He must fully have your heart. Before God can use you, no matter the vocation, He must fully have your heart.

3

A Look Inward

We must identify cultural boundaries that are in need
of kingdom trespass.
—**Dr. Brian Blount,** *Go Preach!*

What keeps us from seeing and knowing neighbors that are different than ourselves? What are the things that get in the way of loving our neighbors? If you look around and all your neighbors look like you, what is it that is keeping you from finding the beauty of God across dividing lines?

I think there are three main things that get in the way of loving our neighbors and expanding our circles: inattentional blindness, implicit bias, and an aversion to discomfort. In order to see how these are at play in our lives, we need to look inward and understand what is happening on a subconscious level.

***

"Who do you think you're better than?"[12]

The people in the crowd looked back at me completely stunned, if not offended.

"We all think this way," I said to the gathered crowd at Center City Church on a Sunday morning in April 2018. "Whether we want to admit it or not, we all have a way of seeing the world in a certain order. I have had to come to grips with my own biases and preconceived ideas of others that are different than me."

I saw Kiera scribble something in her journal. She stared straight past me and into the exposed rafters of the church auditorium. My attention was drawn to her several times throughout the service. It never seemed like she locked back in to what I was saying.

I noticed Kiera waiting patiently to speak to me at the end of the service.

"Pastor David," she said quietly, "I think a lot of people in the room probably thought about homeless people on the corner asking for money. Maybe they thought of people that are living in poverty. However, I have a completely different perspective."

"I noticed you taking notes during the message," I said. "What was on your mind?"

She paused for a few minutes as her eyes moved toward the floor.

"I think I'm better than every person that fills the top of those buildings." She pointed to the skyscrapers in Uptown Charlotte.

"I work so hard to help others in need, and I am in need myself. But I never realized that in my effort to help others, I have formed an opinion of a bunch of people that I have never met that are wealthy and influential. I think I am better than them because I think they are all greedy." Tears started streaming down her face.

Honestly, I was startled. I had never even considered this perspective.

Kiera was one of the most genuinely loving and caring people in our community. She poured herself out for others in a way that was beautiful and inspiring. As she described her response to the message that day, I felt the urge to check my own heart as well.

"My mind kept going back to your question because I realized that I have been judgmental toward anyone that I meet that has a lot of money. I have a huge desire to love others that are, like me, living in poverty. We are just trying to make it work, and it seems like we can't catch a break. However, if I am going to truly love my neighbors the way that you're saying, I need to open my heart to people that aren't like me."

Who do you think you are better than?

Recognize Inattentional Blindness

Hurricane Florence hovered over Charlotte for several days in 2018. The rain was relentless. The combination of a slow-moving storm and high winds meant trees came down and debris filled our yard. I needed a chainsaw to clear the large tree limbs that had fallen. My neighbor said to me, "Head over to Big Earl's."

"Where?" I asked.

"Big Earl's. It's just around the corner. Best deal in town by a longshot, and he won't sell you a piece of junk. You're going to need a good chainsaw for this project."

I had no clue what he was talking about.

Taking his advice, I took a right out of my neighborhood and a left at the first light. Sure enough, there was a mom and pop tool shop on the left side of the street less than a mile down the road. I picked up a great chainsaw and some incredible stories about our neighborhood in the same visit. I never even knew the shop was there.

Inattentional blindness is a psychological phenomenon that causes you to miss things that are right in front of your eyes. I drove by Big Earl's tool shop countless times on my familiar path home. I never noticed it because I never had a need for a chainsaw until Hurricane Florence parked on top of my neighborhood.

I see Big Earl's shop all the time now.

Inattentional blindness is present when discussing racial and economic inequality. It's something that often keeps us from seeing our neighbors and recognizing their needs. I never knew much about unequal treatment of people of color and people from a lower economic class because, as a middle-class white man living in our culture, I did not need to know. I have had the opportunity to live in this world without having to see through the lens of a person of color, a person living in abject poverty, or a woman trying to navigate a world that has been dominated by male leadership.

However, I started to see inequality everywhere once I started to explore racial, economic, and gender inequalities on my own. The more I read, the more I lament. The more

I learn, the more I am profoundly impacted. The more I listen, the more my heart breaks. The more I recognize my inattentional blindness, the more I can help and support my neighbors.

When I live in a homogeneous bubble, it is easy to be dismissive, easy to turn a blind eye. When I build genuine friendships across dividing lines, I am compelled to listen. When I listen to my friends, I am compelled to advocate for equitable treatment of my neighbors of all backgrounds. When I advocate for equal treatment of my friends, I am advocating for countless people that are experiencing the same things. My inattentional blindness is exposed when I hear the stories of people that I love and trust recount times they have been restricted access to board rooms, leadership teams, scholarships, and promotions.

I cannot advocate if I cannot see, however.

We all have inattentional blindness. What is right in front of you that you cannot or have not needed to see? When the psalmist David prayed that God would search his heart, he found that he needed to repent of sins that he did not even know were present.

Will you do the same?

Acknowledge Implicit Bias

Why did I look down and to the left? I thought to myself.

The church I pastored was intentionally located directly on a dividing line between the rich and the poor. I regularly spoke up about finding friendship across dividing lines. I helped start an organization that aimed to help break generational patterns of poverty. I had even begun a doctoral program at Southeastern University studying racial and economic advocacy.

Yet still, I looked down and to the left.

I was so disappointed.

The day was giving way to night as I was walking down Tryon Street in Uptown Charlotte. I had spent an entire day in the city working alongside my neighbors to advocate for developing an affordable housing strategy for our community. My spirits were high, and I was feeling good about the work we were doing. I saw a young couple walking in the opposite direction and I smiled and waved at them. I didn't know them, but I instinctively thought that we could be friends.

A few moments later, a man came walking from the same direction. His hair was disheveled. He was wearing two backpacks. His brow was furrowed and his face unshaved. Without thinking, I took four steps closer to the street and looked down and to the left.

No eye contact.

My actions made it clear I was not to be bothered.

I took a few more steps before I felt the Holy Spirit stop me in my tracks. I sensed a serious and loving rebuke forming in my soul. *Why would you instinctively feel like you could be friends with the well-dressed couple and intentionally move away from another person that was obviously different from you?* That question unsettled me.

I quickly turned around to see if that man was still near me. He was, but I would have had to run back to him, stop him, and then figure out what I needed to say. What was

I supposed to say? "I'm sorry for ignoring you?" That's the first thing that came to mind. That felt more awkward than helpful to me in the moment. As I was engaged in an internal battle with how to remedy the offense, I looked back up and he was nowhere to be found. I knew I missed my moment.

Perceptions of others are taught to us—either explicitly or implicitly—from a very young age. We form our opinions of each other by the way that we see trusted adults treating each other through our formative years. Thus, we have trouble making eye contact with people that we don't understand.

Implicit bias refers to stereotypes that affect our understanding, actions, and decisions in an unconscious manner. I cannot begin to count how many times people that I loved referred to people of color as "those people." There was usually a disparaging or judgmental comment made in accompaniment of that phrase. I grew up in a community that assessed that poor people had the same access to opportunity as everyone else and that "they needed to learn how to work harder just like we do every day."

We can identify some of our implicit biases by asking these questions:

- Was I raised in a homogeneous setting?
- What words were spoken about people who were different from me when I was a child and teenager by older people that I love and trust?
- What opinions do I have of others that were passed on to me by someone else?

- What group of people makes me feel uncomfortable and why?
- What past experiences have shaped my view of everyone else who is similar to that person or people group?

My reaction to the man innocently walking down Tryon Street was not a conscious decision to protect myself. I viewed him as a threat because my unconscious instinct assessed him based on the past experiences of my life and the biases I was taught. I was not operating out of a spirit of neighborliness in that moment. Not even close.

I missed my opportunity to show love through my actions that evening. A simple smile and wave accompanied by eye contact could have gone a long way. I have made a point, a conscious effort, to make eye contact with people that are unlike me since that day. I have no clue how many people I have offended in my life because of moments like that in which my actions went unchecked. However, from that day forward, I have tried to show love and kindness to anyone walking down the street, not just the people who look like me.

Ever since I started intentionally being more kind, I have been assaulted on Tryon Street exactly zero times. Implicit bias, if left unchecked, will always keep us from seeing one another.

Engage Discomfort

When I've got a massive headache, my body isn't crying out for more Advil.

Most of my headaches come from the fact that I'm not drinking enough water. Instead of figuring out the source of the headache, pain killers are the quickest and easiest way to get comfortable. Masking the pain allows me to get back to whatever was hindered by my splitting headache. However, the source of the pain is still there even though I can't feel the pain.

Pain and discomfort abound in our neighborhoods. It is easier to reach for cultural Advil and mask the source of the pain rather than address the reasons that communities have been divided for generations. When you feel the pangs of inequality and injustice, do you engage the root of the problem, or do you ignore the pangs by masking it with justifications and disassociation? We must choose to engage discomfort with grace and courage. If we do not learn to embrace discomfort, the path forward looks awfully homogeneous.

Our present reality is deeply impacted by the past. If we want our future relationships to include a spirit of neighborliness, we will need to explore uncomfortable moments along the way. Choose to engage or choose to ignore. Once a person learns about inequalities that are embedded into the fabric of American culture, these are the only two available options.

Ibram X. Kendi wrote in his book *How to Be an Antiracist*:

The opposite of "racist" isn't "not racist." It is "antiracist." What's the difference? One endorses either the idea of a racial hierarchy as a racist, or racial equality as an antiracist. One either believes problems are rooted in groups of people, as a racist, or locates the roots of problems in power and policies, as an antiracist.[13]

When you engage with these issues, you fight against injustice; when you ignore these issues, you are actively benefiting from the marginalization of others.

If only two choices exist, are you racist or antiracist? Are you following cultural trends that benefit people who look like you and who are in the same racial class? Are you actively working toward a more equitable expression of oneness in your neighborhood?

The Bible never said that we shouldn't get angry about unequal treatment of neighbors. Jesus literally flipped tables over in the temple in holy anger. He rightly assessed that religious leaders were completely off base in their treatment of neighbors. They were overlooking, pushing aside, and marginalizing people for their own personal gain (Matthew 21:12).

Processing and engaging with matters relating to racial and socioeconomic inequality takes time. You may be compelled to try to take action or use your influence to fix an issue. However, you may do more harm than good if you do not take the time to listen, learn, and grow in your own heart first. Tension is accompanied by discomfort. Discomfort leads to prayer, repentance, and growth. Engage discomfort. Embrace it and learn from it. It has a lot to teach you.

When you start to look inward and recognize that the prejudice you have plays into the injustice in the world, it can feel really heavy and uncomfortable. Engaging with this discomfort, rather than ignoring it, will lead to exponential growth and a depth of love that heals dividing lines. Engaging discomfort takes vulnerability and courage.

Would you be willing to be uncomfortable if you knew healing was within reach?

Practice Vulnerability

The road was blurred by the tears streaming from my eyes. I arrived at Crane's Roost Lake to walk and pray. I was so in love with Dara, but with each step I took around the lake, I became more convinced that I couldn't go on with the relationship.

Fear paralyzed my willingness to move forward any further. I made the call that I had nervously rehearsed all day long. "Dara," I said, "I love you more than I've ever loved anyone, but I can't do this. I'm too scared."

The more I opened my heart to Dara, the more uncomfortable I got in my own skin. Instead of courageously addressing the anxiety and fear that was ravaging my soul, I chose to give up. I had her engagement ring in my pocket the night I broke her heart.

My self-preservation plan only lasted one week. I called her back as the familiar feelings of anxiety and fear were raging. "I'm still scared," I said, "But my love for you is stronger than my fear." Clenching her ring in my hand, I asked, "Will you take me back?"

We were married six months later.

We are still married today.

Intimacy can be beautiful and terrifying. There is no feeling in the world like experiencing genuine closeness with someone. The path toward intimacy with a close friend or spouse, however, can never exclude vulnerability. Fear is the enemy of intimacy and is never a trustworthy motive in relationships. You are going to have to embrace vulnerability if you are ever going to genuinely build friendships.

It is not easy when you realize that your actions have led to harm or pain to one of your friends. The easiest thing to do is pack up your heart, go back to the safety of isolation, and never mature. C.S. Lewis beautifully described the need for vulnerability in relationships. He said:

> To love at all is to be vulnerable. Love anything and your heart will be wrung and possibly broken. If you want to make sure of keeping it intact you must give it to no one, not even an animal. Wrap it carefully round with hobbies and little luxuries; avoid all entanglements. Lock it up safe in the casket or coffin of your selfishness. But in that casket, safe, dark, motionless, airless, it will change. It will not be broken; it will become unbreakable, impenetrable, irredeemable. To love is to be vulnerable.[14]

We must wisely choose who receives the gift of intimate friendship in our lives. When you find a trustworthy friend, you will instinctively feel hesitation the first time you are asked to be vulnerable.

"How did you feel when another black man was killed

by police last week?"

That was one of the most terrifying questions that I asked one of my black friends a few years ago. I didn't know if he would be willing to go to that place with me. My heart broke as he described feelings of desperation and exasperation. I felt the tenderness of his trust that was being placed in my care. I resolved in my spirit to do everything I could to the best of my ability to care well for the gift he gave me that day.

God expressed intimacy toward us by sending Jesus to earth. Eugene Peterson says that God became flesh and "moved into the neighborhood" (John 1:14, MSG) We are called to observe His life, learn from His teaching, and embody the presence of Jesus in our neighborhoods. Jesus calls us to an intimate relationship with Him in John 15. He says that He is the vine and we are the branches, that our lives will bear great fruit if we remain in Him. The closeness of our relationship with Jesus will lead us to a healthy expression of closeness with others. As you think through ways to practice vulnerability, consider starting with these questions.

- Who do you know that is from a different racial or economic background than you with whom you can be completely vulnerable?
- If you can immediately think of someone, thank God for them. If you cannot think of anyone, ask that God would expand your circle of friendships in order to see the beauty and strength that is found in diversity.

In order to practice vulnerability, our desire to engage must be stronger than our fear. Second Timothy 1:7 says, "God has not given us a spirit of fear or timidity, but of power, love, and self-discipline." Paul is telling us that God has not given us a spirit of fear and timidity. However, both emotions consistently ravage relationships.

We cannot simply wish away fear and timidity. Those two emotions are extremely real. We feel them viscerally when our heart rate rises during uncomfortable conversations. We feel timidity when we are unsure of what we should say in tense settings. Fear and timidity keep people from asking questions that will explore a complicated history between racial and economic groups in our country.

When this passage from 2 Timothy is applied to our friendships, we can see that God has not given us a spirit of fear or timidity in our friendships. He has given us power to move past our insecurities, love for each other that compels us to know others and be known, and a disciplined mind that chooses to rest in the knowledge that God has intended for us to find friendships across dividing lines. Knowing that God equips us, we can engage discomfort with courage.

Walk in Courage

"We are going to share heaven, let's try to figure out earth."

Thomas and Jamal had a misunderstanding that led to sharp conflict. Six months had passed. A friendship forged over ten years in ministry together was totally fractured, and fear kept the two friends apart. They had disagreed on several things. Jamal believed that Thomas' actions were racially motivated. Thomas was offended because he felt like Jamal was accusing him of being a racist. Imaginary conversations in their heads made both of them believe that the other would never be willing to do the hard work of retracing their steps and finding a common place to stand.

Thomas had typed out his text but stared at the message for several minutes before finally hitting the send button.

"We are going to share heaven, let's try to figure out earth." To his relief and delight, Jamal wrote back within moments.

"When can you meet up?" Thomas asked.

"How about today?" Jamal replied.

They met at a coffeehouse later that afternoon and humbly walked through the various ways both of them could have navigated the friendship better. They admitted errors in the way they handled things. They both asked for and received forgiveness. They found healing. That simple act of courage from both Thomas and Jamal unlocked a beautiful conversation that continues to this day.

A simple text message was the start of a healing conversation. Their reward for embracing discomfort and finding courage to have a hard conversation was healing, forgiveness, and unity. When we are fearful of a situation and feeling weak, we can lean into God's strength to give us courage to push forward. Is there someone that you need to text today?

***

Embracing discomfort in the things that God has called us

to do means embracing His promises as well. He will always be with us. He will not lead us into moments that are greater than we can bear with Him by our side. I am never alone because God is always with me. You are never alone.

Courage is not a result of how strong we are, but rather an admission that we need God to be our strength. The apostle Paul even said that he is at is strongest in the spirit when he is at his weakest in the flesh (2 Corinthians 12:8–10). Paul is literally begging God to take away his weakness, and God's reply is simple: I am strongest when you are weak.

We have an entire history to work through in order to truly embrace one another across racial and economic lines. We cannot do this in our own strength. We need to ask God to search our hearts, to know us, to see if there is any offensive way in us, and to lead us to Him (Psalm 139:23–24). Inattentional blindness and implicit bias are things we need to look out for as we seek to understand our neighbors' experiences. Once our eyes have been opened, we can't unsee; we can either ignore or engage. If we want our communities to flourish, we must engage and embrace discomfort with vulnerability and courage.

Looking inward and becoming aware of the prejudices present in our hearts can be overwhelming at times and comes with a lot of discomfort. But the healing of dividing lines cannot be done without this first step of looking inward. Embracing discomfort means feeling the pangs of injustice without trying to mask the pain. It means laying down our weapons of words and finding healing in the words of Jesus. He calls us to love each other as we would want to be loved. Jesus spent extravagant amounts of time with people that were different from Him. He met them where they were, listened to them, and empathized with them. If we want to look like Him, we should do the same.

It's okay to feel the pain if we believe the healer is with us.

4

Reconsidering
Reconciliation and Inclusion

We're not trying to get back to a place of harmony, but
to a new place where we can be together today.
—Mark Charles, *Unsettling Truths*

I think we need to reconsider using the word *reconciliation.*

Don't get me wrong, I am all for work along the lines
of racial reconciliation. However, the more I explore these
topics and find friendship across racial lines, the more I
think we may not have a healthy beginning to which we
can return. After all, reconciliation means *to restore friendship or harmony.*

To which point in American history would we return
that was equitable and just toward people of color? To which
point would we return that was healthy, unified, and expressing the oneness that God has intended for each person
created in His image? To which point would we return that
was equitable for brilliant teenagers who live in high-pover-

ty neighborhoods as opposed to their higher-income peers?

Answer: there is not a time in our history that is not marked by oppression of a minority group. Our country was founded by acquiring land by manipulation, violence, and aggression toward Native Americans. Soong-Chan Rah and Mark Charles wrote a stunning book called *Unsettling Truths* that meticulously walks the reader through incredibly upsetting and well documented truths about the forceable way in which America was founded on land we did not own. The opening line of chapter one is, "You cannot discover lands already inhabited."[15]

Rah also wrote a book called *Many Colors* that paints a startling picture of the history of the United States. He said:

> There is no denying the long and well documented history of racism in America: the kidnapping of slaves from Africa and the removal of their human identity; the violation of numerous treaties with the Native American community; the genocide of Native American cultures and their peoples; the assumptions of manifest destiny that led to the conquering of Native lands and intervention in Latin America; the exclusion of certain people groups from having the opportunity to immigrate to the United States; the imposition of laws that discriminated in job opportunities and education; the internment of the Japanese community, many of whom were American citizens; Jim Crow laws that maintained an imbalanced power dynamic.[16]

The sheer volume of this list is overwhelming. And it is only a partial list of offenses.

Furthermore, the church has been engaged in the same

behaviors as the predominant culture since the foundation of our country. Jemar Tisby gave a stunning overview of the church's complicity in racism in his book *The Color of Compromise.* He said, "Historically speaking, when faced with the choice between racism and equality, the American church has tended to practice a complicit Christianity rather than a courageous Christianity. They chose comfort over constructive conflict and in so doing created and maintained a status quo of injustice."[17]

Think of reconciliation through the lens of a person of color in our country and in our churches. If we are a country built upon the principles of a predominantly white culture, how do you think it sounds to a person of color when we talk about reconciliation? Exactly what are we returning to that would bring healing?

We need to consider exploring conversations that bring *racial conciliation.*

Mark Charles said, "Reconciliation assumes a pre-existing harmony in the relationship. Conciliation is simply defined as *the mediation of a dispute.* Racial reconciliation perpetuates the myth of America but racial conciliation acknowledges the broken history of race in our nation."[18] Significant and meaningful steps toward racial conciliation can be accomplished by folks who have grown up in the dominant culture taking the time to humbly listen, learn, and grow in our understanding of what it's like to be a person of color in our country.

We need to ask better questions instead of giving quick answers to societal problems that, if we're really honest, we probably don't understand in the first place.

- Why are people of color imprisoned four times more than white people in America?
- Why are prison sentences for similar crimes longer for people of color than white people?
- Why did the "war on drugs" target predominantly black and high-poverty communities?
- Why are there four times the amount of people of color in our prisons than were ever in slavery?
- Why has our country never truly made amends with Native Americans who are living in oppression to this day?[19]

There are so many questions we can ask such as these would heighten our awareness and bring understanding between friends. However, if we're not willing to ask questions, we will never truly be ready to understand our neighbors. If we do not aim to understand our neighbors, we can never truly love our neighbors. If we cannot truly love our neighbors, we cannot fulfill the most important commandment.

***

"I have to be honest, James, I hate the word inclusion."

James looked at me with a mixed reaction of shock, disappointment, and confusion. After all, he was the leader of the newly formed diversity and inclusion group at a very large organization. The group was doing great work creating safe places for people to have conversations about realities along racial and gender lines that are present within a predominantly white and male-led organization.

I replied, "Let me explain. You know I love the work you guys are doing. However, I hate that word because of the implications that go along with it."

"Ok, I'm intrigued," he said.

The word inclusion implies that there is a dominant group of people *allowing* a minority group to participate in the dominant expression of the organization. This can include one dominant race, economic status, or gender. That doesn't sound like much fun, does it?

Think about your workplace, church, or an organization you're involved with on a consistent basis. Is there one dominant race in significant leadership positions? Is there one dominant gender in those same roles?

I spend a lot of time with organizations that are led by all-male and all-white executive teams. Executive and corporate cultures are missing out on so much brilliance and beauty by filling rooms with people who look and act like one another. In order to truly love one another well, we need to take the time to understand and see one another, appreciate one another, and make room for more perspectives.

A dominant group has a certain expression of the way they see the world, experience their faith, and make decisions. When a person of color or a woman is invited to be *included* in an organization that is led by a predominantly white and male leadership team, many times that simply means they have been invited to help the dominant group continue to express their monotone worldview without genuine input in the final decision. If a person in the margins is not given the opportunity to make decisions or give input that would be deeply considered, inclusion comes off as disingenuous at best and grossly oppressive at worst. In order to truly experience the beauty of diversity, there has to be decision makers in the room that come from various backgrounds.

How can an all-white board of directors make decisions that truly make people of color feel like their organization is allowing them to operate from their true center if no one looks like them in the room? How can an all-male executive team make a well-informed decision for the women in that company without any women present?

Let's dig in a bit more to church culture. Simply diversifying the *racial representation* of the worship team does not actually mean you've created an atmosphere that is creating space for people of color to worship from their true center. If every song that is played on a Sunday morning is from the same general genre from the dominant culture, the expression of worship from folks who have lived in the margins may never genuinely connect on a heart level. We have to learn how to sing together, even if the songs aren't familiar or preferred.

We have to become more committed to filling executive teams, board rooms, and worship teams with women and people of color who are brilliant, qualified, and bring much-needed perspective to a white and male-dominated culture. If you have a position of influence within an organization that is dominated by a single ethnic or gender group, how can you use that influence to highlight the qualification and brilliance of people that have been pushed to the margins?

Austin Channing Brown said in her book, *I'm Still Here*:

> Without people of color in key positions, influencing topics of conversation, content, direction, and vision, whatever diversity is included is still essentially white—it just adds people of color like sprinkles on top. The cake is still vanilla.

Inattentional blindness may have led you to never acknowledge that your organization was dominated by one race or gender. This phenomenon means that you get so used to your surroundings that you miss things in that context that are obvious to others.

Most of my white friends genuinely hire the best people they *know.* I believe that to be true. However, that also probably means that they are hiring a lot of white people in executive positions because their circles of friendship do not include many people of color. Expanding your circle of friendship also expands your circle of creativity and brilliance and brings in perspectives that enrich your life and value to organizations.

There are brilliant folks all around who are different from you. That being said, there are practical ways you can explore moving forward in new ways. Start by analyzing the context of your life and friendships. Who are your friends and the people who join you during your lunch break? Which friends enjoy evening conversations in your living room?

Auditing your life and friendships begins to open your eyes to the reality that there's a much broader expression of beauty and brilliance than what we have experienced in a largely homogeneous and divided culture.

I don't want to invite people who are different from me to assimilate and express themselves from my perspective. I want to experience the beauty of God the way I see in Revelation 7:9, "I saw a huge crowd, too huge to count. Everyone was there—all nations and tribes, all races and languages" (MSG). An entire community was singing and worshiping God with one voice. We all don't have to sing the same part to sing the same song. Harmony—the combination of different notes—is what makes for a beautiful song.

Is your church, nonprofit, or business singing a beautiful song? Or is it monotone? Have you invited a group of talented singers to sing the same part you learned?

I have heard beautiful songs of diversity. The melodies and harmonies are breathtaking and beautiful. It will take some practice, but let's choose to sing together. Inclusion does not equal diversity.

"I see you, David," James said to me laughing. "I didn't know where you were going with that one but I see you now. Let's sing together."

★★★

If you are struggling with this chapter, take a moment and just pause. Where is your discomfort coming from?

Are you more concerned about disagreeing with the content of this chapter or the fear of addressing issues of the heart? When you choose to follow Jesus, He leads you directly into relationship with people who are not like you. Try to put yourself, your feelings, and your political beliefs aside for a moment. Open up your heart. Feel the pain that others have felt for generations. Let your heart break so compassion can enter through the cracks. Learn to love by learning to see, feel, and hear the experiences of your neighbors.

Reconciliation can only happen if we have a place to which we can return. If we are going to return to something, let's go all the way back to the story of Jesus. He showed us how to open our arms, invite everyone to the table, and enjoy a diverse community of friendship and oneness. His life radiated the spirit of neighborliness.

To my white friends: I want to humbly listen, learn, and grow. I need to humbly listen, learn, and grow. I invite you to do the same. Let's start by doing some work of learning on our own and choosing to acknowledge that something is wrong. We have put the burden of proof on our neighbors who have been overlooked, pushed aside, and marginalized for too long. Let's care about our neighbors enough to look past our own perspective. When we learn the true stories of our history, we can engage in conciliatory conversations that bring healing that has never been realized in American culture.

A great place to start exploring our culture from the perspective of a person of color is a Netflix documentary called *13TH*. This documentary explores how the prison system has been skewed to be filled with people of color. The Thirteenth Amendment, which many understand to have abolished slavery, introduced a new system that became a more subtle way to oppress people of color and people in lower economic classes.

Michelle Alexander's book *The New Jim Crow: Mass Incarceration in the Age of Colorblindness* is one step deeper into the topic of race, economics, and the American prison system. I could not believe how much I did not know about my neighbors. Honestly, I had to repent of not caring. I always just assumed that people who ended up in jail somehow deserved to end up there. I couldn't have been more wrong.

Additionally, I did not understand that white folks, including myself, are moving along as if nothing is wrong while people of color are required to live with the imbalance of our culture on a daily basis.

Before we can have racial reconciliation, we need to start with conciliation. And in order to experience conciliation, there is some unlearning and listening that we must do. Dr. Len Sweet said, "All learning requires unlearning, which requires tremendous courage." I pray that we would have tremendous courage as we reconsider reconciliation and inclusion.

5

From One Generation to the Next

My work is to give you what I know of my own
particular path while allowing you to walk your own.
—Ta-Nehisi Coates, *Between the World and Me*

The thing I've found that speaks the most in our relationships with people is intentionality. The way I see this playing out the most in my life is through parenting. Dara and I love our babies (they will always be our babies) so very much. They bring so much joy to our lives. Max, Mary, Jack, and Ben are my kids, my best friends, and my greatest teachers.

Parenting has been one of the biggest blessings in my life, but parenting can be straight up hard. Dara and I are imperfect at the art of parenting, but we care deeply. We are intentional with our kids in our conversations, our discipline, our teaching moments, and our schedules. Pursuing intentionality is far greater than striving for perfection because it allows for curiosity, mistakes without shame, and deeper connections with people in your community.

Whether you are married, single, with kids, or without, I want to share with you how Dara and I are exploring sensitive and complex topics with our children. My prayer is that you will pick up some practices along the way of how we can pass on important lessons from one generation to the next. I want the same thing for you that I want for my kids. I want you to fix your attention on what Jesus said was most important: loving God and neighbors.

Everything else, after all, is less important.

Sitting with Our Neighbors

"Welcome to Woolworth's lunch counter."

Maugrette, our guide for the day at the National Center for Civil and Human Rights in Atlanta, directed us to step into a recreation of a 1950's diner. She had an engaging smile and an obvious passion for her job. Her thick-rimmed glasses could not conceal the joy that was present in her eyes on that cold January morning in Atlanta.

The bar top was accompanied by four metal barstools with red cushioned seats. Four noise-canceling headphones were attached to the bar in front of each stool. Still images of a dozen white men and two black men sitting at the original diner in Greensboro, North Carolina were illuminated on a screen that stretched the length of the bar.

"We ask that anyone under the age of twelve abstain from participating in this experience," Maugrette told a crowd of twenty people.

I stayed back with our eleven-year-old son, Ben, as Dara and our teenagers stepped into the diner and placed the headphones on their ears. A red timer appeared on a screen in front of Dara and the kids.

"Please close your eyes," Maugrette said. "The experience lasts ninety seconds. If you need to, however, you can take the headphones off at any time."

If you need to?

In combination with the fact that they asked Ben not to participate, that bit of information struck me as curious. I stood about five feet away from Jack, our thirteen-year-old, and observed. He grimaced after about five seconds. Ten seconds later, his face was scrunched up in the same way he tried not to show pain when he broke his finger during a playoff basketball game. Thirty seconds into the experience, he took the headphones off, looked at me with tears forming in his eyes, and said, "Dad, I didn't like that." I hugged him, curious as to what he just experienced.

Dara, Max, and Mary sat stoically as the clock counted down and hit triple zeros.

"Wow," Max said as he placed the headphones on the counter. "That was intense."

Mary quietly pulled her headphones off and walked a few steps away from the counter. Her arms were crossed, and her gaze was fixed on an empty black wall ten feet away. It was obvious to me that she was staring at the memories that just entered her mind.

Dara immediately made a beeline for Jack. "Are you ok, my love?"

She wrapped her arms around him. Jack settled into a

loving embrace that is uniquely reserved for a mother and son. I observed my wife and teenage kids experience a moment I had never seen and did not understand.

I stepped up to the counter, picked up the headphones, and took a deep breath. I placed the headphones over my ears and the sounds of the world quickly subsided. I could hear the familiar sounds of any restaurant I have ever enjoyed. Eyes closed, I heard forks and knives on plates and muffled conversations.

The door to the diner opened over my right shoulder. The diner became quiet for a brief moment.

Get out of here!

You don't belong here!

The voices came closer to my bar stool.

YOU! You're just a colored-people lover!

You're just as bad as any one of them colored people!

I could hear the sounds of multiple men surrounding me and whomever I was dining with at Woolworth's Lunch Counter that afternoon. The shouts became more aggressive, including extremely inappropriate and uncomfortable threats and disparaging comments. I peeked at the clock in front of me.

Thirty seconds had passed.

The shouts grew louder and came from every angle. Over my left shoulder, behind me, and over my right shoulder, the insults were hurled mercilessly and viciously. Eyes closed, I was immersed in a scenario as a white man sitting with my black friends at a white-only diner.

WHACK! My barstool violently shook as the sound of someone unexpectedly punching my left ear screamed through the headphones.

I said get out of here!

THUMP! POP! Two more violent shakes from the bar stool accompanied two more punches to my right and left ears.

This is just the beginning!

You think it is okay to sit here with colored people?

We'll be waiting for you outside. There's more of where this came from for you!

An entire crowd of people were verbally and physically assaulting my imaginary friend and me at Woolworth's lunch counter. I opened my eyes to see the clock tick down. *Three, two, one.*

I removed my headphones and stared forward in a bit of a daze. A grainy video of actual footage from Woolworth's lunch counter played in front of me. People sitting at a lunch counter with courage and resolve. They absorbed physical assault, public scorn, and food poured over their heads. Maugrette informed us that this scenario unfolded in countless diners across the country during the 1950s and 1960s. Far worse things happened than what this family-friendly museum could recreate.

That felt very real, I thought to myself. I no longer wondered why Jack removed his headphones and stepped away from the bar. I was viscerally shaken. My kids were shaken. The time came to move on with our guided tour. I looked at my kids and fought back tears. Knowing that they had just experienced something emotional and jarring, I instinctively knew we had to take a moment before moving on with our tour. The kids could not immediately move on from this moment. Dara and I couldn't either. I asked Maugrette if I could have a moment with my wife and kids. We had to talk about what we had experienced.

I leaned in and asked, "What are you guys thinking about after experiencing that?" The kids looked at me with stunned sadness in their eyes.

"I didn't like it, Dad," Jack said again. Dara still had him in a loving and protective embrace.

"I'm thinking that I'm glad they didn't let me do it," Ben quipped.

"I know that was hard to experience," I said. "However, did you know that people actually experienced that in our country?"

The kids quietly nodded.

"I have a question I keep asking myself after sitting at that lunch counter. I want to ask you the same question, but you do not need to answer me right now. Would you sit with one of your friends at that counter?"

Silence.

***

I was just as uncomfortable as my kids when I sat at that counter. I was emotional during and after the experience. The words that followed were not eloquent. I wasn't prepared to lead an emotional teaching moment. However, looking into the eyes of my kids, I knew God would give me the words to say as I intentionally used this moment to help their minds process what they were experiencing.

Parenting is hard. I constantly question whether I'm doing things right. During this specific moment, I wondered if we unintentionally exposed them to something that was too viscerally stimulating. And then I remembered that kids are resilient. I was reminded that they have seen more in their time on this earth than Dara and I even know about. The thought of that reality pains me deeply.

Our experience at Woolworth's lunch counter was different, though. We were together. We shared an uncomfortable and painful experience as a family. Although none of us were prepared, we could navigate the next steps together. But, someone needed to take the lead and help them process what they had just experienced.

I didn't know what to say, so we sat quietly for a few minutes. However, the simple act of leading our family through a hard conversation turned out to be beautiful. The reality is that we will most likely never have to make that decision to sit at a counter while our friends are being publicly attacked. Racism is often more subtle these days. But it is still present in countless ways. The equivalent question of whether or not we would sit with a friend at Woolworth's lunch counter might be:

- Will you stand up for a friend when inappropriate racial comments are made and everyone in your friend group is laughing?
- Will you speak up in the board room when the weights and balances of racial equity are not equally measured?
- Will you have the courage to call out inappropriate behaviors of people you love if

their behavior is causing division, pain, or harm
to people of another race or economic status?

The National Center for Civil and Human Rights not
only provided an educational opportunity for me and my
family, it gave us language and experiences that we could not
have curated on our own. These honest and difficult conversations led to beautiful moments of vulnerability and courage that helped our family learn and grow. We were given
the opportunity to consider things that were outside of our
normal rhythm and routine.

We grew as individuals. We grew as a family.

A bit of intentionality goes a long way.

Without educating ourselves, we can't really know
our neighbors who experience discrimination and racism.
Without knowing our neighbors, we can't stand with them.
Without standing with our neighbors, we can't really love
them.

Initiating Hard Conversations

During our trip to Atlanta, Dara and I were able to have
open and honest conversations with our kids about some
really tough parts of human history. The alternative to moments like this is to simply let the kids develop their own
thoughts and perspectives.

My kids see what is happening on the news. They know
that Keith Lamont Scott was killed twenty minutes from
our home. They saw the images on their phones of people

throwing bricks through windows of familiar buildings during protests in our city.

I am not protecting them by avoiding hard conversations about Woolworth's lunch counter, Keith Lamont Scott's death, or protests in our city. Avoiding issues does not lead to growth. By addressing these difficult conversations, I am teaching them how to navigate the world with grace, courage, and strength. Remember, they are going to see terrible things whether I am there to talk to them or not. I want to be the one who talks to my kids about the complexity of life. I want to create a safe place for them to ask hard questions, even if I don't know the answers. I want to point them to the hope and love that is found in Jesus. I want to help shape their heart, mind, and spirit to celebrate differences, not fear someone who is different.

A huge part of the privilege of parenting is the opportunity to engage in conversations with your kids. Courage and curiosity go hand in hand when exploring the pain, hardship, and difficulty of the world. There is no better person to answer curious questions than a parent who has built a loving and trusting relationship with their child. Proverbs 22:6 says, "Direct your children onto the right path, and when they are older, they will not leave it." We cannot guarantee what our children will do or become. However, we can choose to do all we can to direct them onto the right path.

Priorities

Shannon is a small business owner and the mother of three teenage girls.

She loves her girls.

A normal week includes waking up at 6:05 a.m. each day, throwing together a quick breakfast for the girls, and rushing out the door by 7:00 a.m. to get everyone to school on time. After working a full day and navigating all the joys and challenges of owning a business, she fights the traffic on Randolph Road to get the girls home from school and started on their homework. The crockpot has become her best friend because it has been doing the cooking most of the day and allows her to finish up some final work things before starting the side dishes for dinner. The crockpot is replaced by Postmates on especially busy days.

Tuesday evening is youth group for the kids. Lacrosse practice is on Monday and Wednesday. Soccer practices are Wednesday and Thursday. At least three games take place each Saturday. Shannon and the girls are also actively involved at their church, when they can make it, of course.

Shannon and I have been friends for over twenty years, and we were recently talking about the importance of healing the dividing lines in our culture.

"David, I am totally with you. I want my girls to grow up knowing how to connect across dividing lines. But I live in the suburbs, and literally every single person in our neighborhood is white," she continued. "Go outside right now and just look around. There's not a single family of color in this neighborhood. I didn't intentionally choose that, it's just the way the neighborhood naturally formed."

I could hear the slightest tone of defensiveness in her voice. But curiosity was the most discernable emotion that I picked up on as we were talking.

"I work really hard to make sure I provide for my kids, and all three of them are involved in sports and church." She was cutting the celery on her marble countertop a bit harder as the conversation continued.

"Tell me," she inquired sincerely, "how am I supposed to teach my girls how to express a spirit of neighborliness when we don't have time to spend with the friends we already have in the first place?" She continued, "Everyone in our area is either upper-middle class or wealthy. Do you expect me to drive them forty-five minutes south into downtown on the weekends to hang out with poor people?"

She paused after that final comment.

"That didn't come out right. I don't mean to be rude or defensive. I am just being honest. I don't really know what to do. I want to raise my girls right, but our lives are so busy."

I cannot count how many times I have had conversations like this one with Shannon. Parents instinctively want to raise their kids to experience a full and satisfying life. I tell my kids all the time that I pray that God gives them double of anything He's ever done for me or given to me in my lifetime.

However, I have also observed that parents can get paralyzed with unreasonable shame and disappointment if they look at the context of their lives and realize that it is predominantly homogeneous. It is a very normal occurrence to find common ground with people who are similar to us.

Communities are largely organized by similar economic groups. Neighborhoods regularly include a dominant majority of a particular ethnic group.

Shannon isn't wrong.

Life can get so busy that there is barely enough time to cultivate even a few meaningful relationships. The thought of trying to navigate the minefield of relationships across dividing lines can be overwhelming. The temptation to continue navigating the familiar world, which has enough challenges to keep all of us busy, persists. Why choose to introduce more complexity?

The thought of disrupting the rhythm of life that has taken so much time and intentionality to construct can be daunting. However, this does not excuse us as parents from raising holistic and healthy kids. Parents need to expose their children to things that will lead to maturity and fullness in their relationship with Jesus. Figuring out how to navigate relationships across dividing lines is a primary responsibility for parents who want to raise well-rounded kids.

"Shannon," I said, "there are so many things we need to focus on as we raise our kids. If we are going to cut things out of our lives to prioritize the most important things, let's make sure that what Jesus said was most important is not on the chopping block."

***

The more you learn as a parent, the more you are able to pass on to your kids. Raising your children to love God and neighbors with full passion is a primary responsibility. However, it will never be a priority in your parenting if it is not a priority in your heart.

My journey started with a book called *Trouble I've Seen: Changing the Way the Church Views Racism* by Drew Hart.[20] This was the very first book I read when we were considering moving our church from the predominantly white Elizabeth neighborhood to the predominantly black Camp Greene neighborhood. That day in church when my eyes were opened, my next step wasn't to try to teach my kids about systemic racism or matters that, quite honestly, I didn't know enough about to even carry on a substantive conversation. I started by asking some friends what I could read that would help me understand some of the dynamics better. Hart's book was incredibly helpful to me because he shared intimate and personal stories about being a black man raised in the evangelical church.

I can't say it was an easy read, but it was important. The difficulty was due to preconceived ideas that were being challenged in my heart by a man who courageously told his story. The more I digested on my own, the more I was able to instinctively start bringing up conversations with my kids. I learned pretty quickly that my kids had quite a bit more interaction with people of color than I did because of their schools. And they didn't have thirty-five years of experiences that added up to a mostly homogeneous life.

They were way more open to questions I had about their experiences at school than I thought they would be when I first started exploring these matters myself. As I continued to learn, the conversations at home became more frequent.

Discussions about things we saw on the news or things that happened at school became more natural and regular. We all have a choice as to what we will choose to learn about and discuss with our families. And we chose to start having more conversations about race and different economic classes.

My kids never scoffed at the questions the way some of my older friends did. "David, are you seriously bringing this up again?" That is a common question among adults who are more set in their ways, but I noticed that my kids were still full of curiosity and openness to the various expressions of life and community that filled their world. Simply put, I was more afraid of the conversations about race and economics than they were. I just needed to have the courage and intentionality to engage in meaningful conversation. However, if I was going to intentionally bring up conversation with them, I had to keep learning on my own. My kids have helped me to see that if I am willing to explore topics that are uncomfortable, painful, or complex, they are willing to go there with me.

***

Studies have shown a global trend where cities are rapidly growing. We have reached the point that 50 percent of the world population now lives in cities, as compared to 5 percent two centuries ago.[21] This number will continue to rise as the world moves toward large population centers around the globe.

The rich and the poor are neighbors in cities.

The nations of the world congregate in cities.

When you choose to discuss race and economics with your kids, you are preparing them to navigate life in the real world. You don't have to move into a new neighborhood or drive forty-five minutes to volunteer at a food pantry in a high-poverty community to teach them the spirit of neighborliness. You can use the same creativity and intentionality that creates fun family memories to find engaging ways to spark meaningful conversations about race and economics. Your courage and creativity will set the example in your home of loving God and neighbors. But you have to be willing to learn before you will be prepared to teach.

Everyone knows that we need to teach our kids how to brush their teeth, tie their shoes, and drive a car. Most parents teach their kids to say *please, thank you, yes sir, yes ma'am,* and *I'm sorry.* We do this because we want to teach our kids how to function in the world. Here are some other practices you can implement.

- Prepare your children to inhabit the real world by teaching them to embrace the beauty of the diversity of God as expressed through the diversity of His children.
- Create memories and experiences that explore the topics of race and economics.
- Teach them to ask great questions when they meet new people.
- Cultivate their spirit of curiosity.
- Take them on a trip, have a blast, and choose to take them to a significant and historic location that will spark meaningful conversations.

- Stay curious. Listen, learn, and grow. Pass on what you are learning.

Parenting is not easy, but it is a huge privilege. Your courage will result in courageous kids who engage their world with grace, love, kindness, curiosity, and joy. Your kids are more aware of what's happening than you realize. Choose to be the one who helps them navigate complex conversations. They are talking to someone about what they are seeing online and in the news.

Might as well be you, right?

6

Learning to Lament

Our ransacked world is crying out for the restoration of
the governance of God and the shalom it brings.
—**Lisa Sharon Harper,** *The Very Good Gospel*

I watched a cinder block fly through the window of another building in Uptown Charlotte. Police dressed in riot gear formed a wall with bulletproof shields. The crowd was swelling and the situation was growing more tense by the minute.

Protesters chanted, "No justice, no peace!"

"Stop killing us!"

"Justice for Keith Lamont Scott!"

I was 550 miles from home the night Charlotte, North Carolina erupted. Through the television in my hotel room, I watched the city I love and call home cry out for justice. The vast majority of the people on the streets were peacefully protesting the death of a black man, Keith Lamont Scott, at the hands of police on September 20, 2016. A small group of people, however, threw rocks, water bottles, and anything else they could find at police and at the skyrise buildings.

I saw my friends on CNN—people that I know and love. New friends who had welcomed our church family into the West Charlotte community when we moved from Elizabeth. They were among the crowds of people demanding justice. And I was three states away. I wanted so badly to be on the streets with my friends that evening.

I doubled over on the couch of my room at the Hampton Inn in Lakeland, Florida. Tears were accompanied by prayers. I was crying with my friends.

Insulated from Pain

I was twelve years old when I started to hear news of a man named Rodney King who was assaulted on the streets of Los Angeles. I vaguely remembered watching the news and seeing a black man being relentlessly kicked, punched, and beaten by four police officers. I had no context for what was happening, but I remember feeling as though it was way over the line.

I started seeing reports on the news about riots that were happening in Los Angeles because the police officers involved in the incident were not charged with a crime. I distinctly remember this, but nothing hit my emotional radar.

"We didn't see what Rodney King did before the video."

"He was drinking all night long before the cops showed up."

"Can you believe people would destroy a city because of one man that was in an altercation with police?"

These were the type of responses I remember hearing from the adults in my life. No one took the time to talk with me about the cultural climate that led to these events. I was far away and insulated from the realities that led to these protests in the streets of Los Angeles.

I was thirty-two years old the night Trayvon Martin was killed fifteen minutes from where I grew up in the suburbs of Orlando, Florida. I was married and had four kids under the age of eight years old. I was bothered by the reports describing a seventeen-year-old young man that was killed by a self-imposed neighborhood watch guard. Dara and I watched the news and we couldn't believe that something like this happened in a neighborhood so close to where we lived when we were first married. One of my best friends, Ryan, grew up a few minutes from the location of this shooting. I had driven by this neighborhood countless times. Even as a thirty-two-year-old husband, father, and pastor, I was still not lamenting the fact that a young man was killed unnecessarily. I was mostly just shocked that a young man could be killed in a place that was so close to home.

The location of this shooting was close to home, but the reality of this shooting was far away. I did not process this news with any people of color. No one in my relational circle seemed to be emotionally charged either. I had no context to know how to grieve with anyone who was touched by this tragedy. After brief moments of feeling sad for such an unimaginable scenario unfolding, I moved on and continued to plan for the upcoming Sunday service at Center City Church.

***

Eric Garner was killed on July 17, 2014 in Staten Island, New York. Michael Brown was killed on August 9, 2014 in St. Louis, Missouri. Tamir Rice was killed on November 22, 2014 in Cleveland, Ohio. Freddie Gray was killed on April 21, 2015 in Baltimore, Maryland. Alton Sterling was killed on July 5, 2016 in Baton Rouge, Louisiana. Philando Castile was killed on July 6, 2016 just east of Minneapolis, Minnesota.

These are just six examples of black men killed in police-related deaths. I distinctly remember seeing each of these incidents on the news. I didn't shed a single tear. Every one of these instances felt so far away and removed from my daily life.

If I am being completely honest, I also didn't care enough to connect the dots that were forming in my mind. I knew there was a pattern. Police-related deaths and the black community were constantly in the news. But I never grieved. I never explored the questions that were instinctively forming in my head.

It wasn't my problem because my world was not touched by the harsh reality of police-related deaths. I was insulated from the pain, so there was no thought in my mind that I should learn to grieve with my neighbors over the senseless loss of life that continued to happen year after year.

Deep-Seated Dynamics

The weeks following our announcement that Center City Church would be moving from the affluent Elizabeth community southeast of Uptown Charlotte to the historically high-poverty Camp Greene community mere miles away, we lost a quarter of the members of our church.

I was absolutely convinced that the vision for racial and economic equity the Center City Church staff had for the neighborhood would inspire two communities that had been divided for so long to come together. However, many in our predominantly white congregation were not ready for the dynamics that, admittedly, I didn't even know were present when God opened this door. Furthermore, I was beginning to learn that the community that I knew God was calling us to would not simply welcome us with open arms. I learned that many in the community viewed us as yet another predominantly white group coming into a predominantly black community with visions of how to "fix the neighborhood."

The day we moved into our new home at 2225 Freedom Drive, our congregation was half the size it was the day that I announced our move to West Charlotte. I was ecstatic to see the building and vision finally come to life, but I was also heartbroken and exhausted, not simply by the amount of people who left, but the reasons they gave for leaving to find another church home.

I honestly believed that if any church could make this move with grace, wisdom, and strength, it was Center City Church. We had worked so hard over the course of six years to build a genuine and loving community. I was not ready for the reasons so many people were choosing to leave a church they previously loved. The move, after all, was exactly four miles. Little did I know, "The Tale of Two Cities" was about to become painfully clear right in front of me.

"Why are you choosing to ruin a beautiful church by

moving to West Charlotte?"

"I am not sending my kids to childcare in *that* location."

"How are we supposed to be safe in *that* community?"

"*That* community will never accept us, anyway."

I had failed to anticipate the deep-seated dynamics that were present in our church family regarding race and economics. And I had failed to realize these same uncomfortable dynamics were present in my heart as well.

Building Awareness

One of the first cracks in my emotional armor came during the first semester of my doctoral program. I went back to school to explore the cyclical patterns of generational poverty. I was bothered by the fact that many of my new friends in West Charlotte came from families that were living in poverty generation after generation. The location of concentrated poverty bothered me because I could see the skyrise buildings in Uptown Charlotte from the Camp Greene neighborhood. *There's so much opportunity less than a mile away,* I thought to myself.

Dr. Alan Ehler asked us to choose a topic for our first research paper. He suggested that we choose a topic that we may want to shape our entire doctoral program around for the next three years. I chose to write a paper titled "An Overview of Generational Poverty."

When I began my research, Michelle Alexander's book *The New Jim Crow: Mass Incarceration in the Age of Colorblindness* was one of the first books I read.

Alexander described in excruciating detail how communities of color were targeted with excessive arrests as compared to predominantly white communities. She continued by explaining the result of picking up a felony charge in our country. I couldn't hardly believe how naïve and unaware I was regarding these realities. She stated,

> Once you're labeled a felon, the old forms of discrimination—employment discrimination, housing discrimination, denial of the right to vote, denial of educational opportunity, denial of food stamps and other public benefits, and exclusion from jury service—are suddenly legal. As a criminal, you have scarcely more rights, and arguably less respect, than a black man living in Alabama at the height of Jim Crow. We have not ended racial caste in America; we have merely redesigned it.[22]

I was starting to remember events like the war on drugs in the 1980s. I had always thought this was a good thing. How could it be bad to get drugs and drug dealers off our streets? I felt defensive and uncertain about my own understanding of what was clearly being laid out in the book I held in my hands. Alexander went to great lengths to show undeniable discrepancies in arrests of people of color as opposed to arrests for similar crimes in white communities.

I had heard stories about discriminatory sentencing during the war on drugs, but I was now seeing it in indisputable research. My heart dropped when I read Alexander's description of sentences given to people for crack cocaine, a form of cocaine commonly found in high-poverty communities, as opposed to powder cocaine, which is found mainly in middle- to upper-class communities. Crack offenses were being sentenced one hundred times more severely than offenses involving powder cocaine. She said, "A conviction for the salve of five hundred grams of powder cocaine triggers a five-year mandatory sentence, while only five grams of crack triggers the same sentence."[23]

Referencing the skewed percentages toward people of color in the prison system, Alexander stated, "The racial dimension of mass incarceration is its most striking feature. No other country in the world imprisons so many of its racial or ethnic minorities. The United States imprisons a larger percentage of its black population than South Africa did at the height of apartheid."[24] Dominique DuBois Gilliard also highlights the inequalities in the U.S prison system in his book, *Rethinking Incarceration: Advocating for Justice That Restores*. Gilliard states that,

> While the United States constitutes only 5 percent of the world's population, we have 25 percent of its incarcerated populace. Statistically, our nation currently has more locked up—in jails, prisons, and detention centers—than any other country in the history of the world. We currently have more jails and prisons than degree-granting colleges and universities.[25]

Jemar Tisby observed in his book *The Color of Compromise: The Truth About the American Church's Complicity in Racism*, "History demonstrates that racism never goes away; it just adapts."[26] With each book I read, the truth of this statement become more and more apparent.

The deluge of information was overwhelming to my

heart. I thought about my friends, co-workers, classmates, and acquaintances who were impacted deeply by the reality of the things I was reading. I was thirty-seven years old the first time I was moved to tears because of racial and economic division in our country. Never once did I consider having a talk with my kids about how to behave if a police officer pulled them over. However, almost every family I was getting to know in West Charlotte told stories of the talk they had with their kids about how to make sure a police officer did not feel they posed a threat.

The relationships I was forming in West Charlotte unlocked an emotional part of my heart that was being triggered as I read about the unequal representation of people of color in prisons across our country. I never grieved this reality because I never took the time to explore the fleeting thoughts that something seemed off every time I saw another headline on the news about a person of color that was involved in a police-related death.

The reason many white people quickly cast aside conversations about the unequal treatment of people of color as compared to white people in our culture is simple: white people, for the most part, do not have to intentionally consider their interaction with police.

No longer were these issues far away. My friends were close to my heart. Their pain was beginning to be my pain. The more I read, the more I could see the faces of my friends that came from different backgrounds than me.

Soon after, the shooting that took the life of Keith Lamont Scott would bring the reality of police-related shootings much closer to home than I had ever experienced.

Empathy

I cried uncontrollably as the news continued to pour in on the television in my hotel room. I scrolled feverishly through Twitter trying to find any information I could about what was happening in Charlotte. I was three states away and feeling completely helpless.

I had never been so emotionally moved by a police-related shooting. The difference was simple. My friends were impacted, and I could feel their pain. People I cared about openly lamented because generation after generation of black men have been the victim of unnecessarily violent interaction with police.

No longer was this another headline on the evening news to me. My heart was impacted because my friends were impacted. This wasn't a political issue or a point to argue at a dinner party. My friends poured into the streets and cried at the top of their lungs for justice.

As I grieved, I sensed that God was grieving with me. The brokenness of the world that was unfolding on the news did not match the promise of peace and unity that is found in Revelation 21. No more pain. No more tears. No more sickness.

"Why God? *Why?!*"

My silent prayers turned into audible questions.

I was learning the power of lament.

***

Relationships have a way of changing the way we view the

brokenness of the world around us. Brené Brown teaches that empathy means "feeling with people."[27] So long as we are removed from relationships with people and people groups that are different from us, we will never have the emotional capacity to be moved to tears when something unjust leads to harm or death for people groups that are different than ours.

Christian theologian and professor Soong-Chan Rah wrote a masterpiece on the topic of lament called *Prophetic Lament*. I spent two weeks reading and digesting this biblical call to healing through mourning. Rah called pastors to lead their congregations into seasons of lament. This was a radical idea to me at first glance. I was taught growing up that church was a place where we came to celebrate the hope we have found in Jesus. Why would we choose to make everybody incredibly sad at church? No one had ever encouraged me to teach my congregation to properly grieve in a way that would lead to wholeness and health.

As I was learning to come to God through lament, I was learning to mine the depths of my soul for places of longing I had never experienced. I was learning a new language of prayer. There were times when the pain of my sorrow for my brothers and sisters would be found in the force and volume of my words and tears. Other times, I could not muster a word. My shouts of protest and groans of despair over the state of the world around me were accompanied by an ever-growing understanding of God's plans and purposes for our world. Oneness. Unity. Peace. Healing.

There were several moments as I read *Prophetic Lament* when I felt the sting that accompanies loving rebuke. Rah directly addressed pastors in urban communities. He said, "Ministry in the urban context, acts of justice and racial reconciliation require a deeper engagement with the other—an engagement that acknowledges suffering rather than glossing over it."[28]

Rather than glossing over it. That phrase hit me between the eyes.

Is that what we have done in the church? Instead of courageously addressing systemic racism and economic oppression in our culture, have we overlooked and pushed aside issues and grief that people of color are experiencing? Have we been singing songs of celebration to God while our neighbors are privately grieving in their homes? If the church will not teach people how to properly grieve in a way that leads to wholeness and healing, how will we ever experience healing in our communities?

I began to realize why so many of our churches are homogeneous. Predominantly white churches are praising and worshiping and celebrating while rarely entering into the power of lament that is experienced in predominantly black, Hispanic, and Native American gatherings.

A quick glance at the history of non-white worship gatherings will show that there are songs of lament that are common among people of color in our history. Harriet Tubman famously led a group of slaves to freedom through the underground railroad while singing songs of lament and hope. Native American believers called out to God on the Trail of Tears. Hispanic churches are filled with songs that declare hope in Christ in the midst of poverty and pain. They don't gloss over suffering—they fully acknowledge it and have hope. People of color have learned to worship God with maturity and courage in spite of the experiences that they have endured on this earth that have led to brokenness and pain.

If you grew up in a predominantly white church, can you name a single song that is a part of the mainstream culture of worship that inspires us to properly lament in a way that ultimately leads to Jesus? I can think of one.

"It is Well" is a classic hymn that was written by Horatio Spafford after experiencing the tragic loss of his four daughters—Tanetta, Maggie, Annie, and Bessie—in an accident at sea. Spafford penned this classic hymn which declares that his soul is well when he fixes his attention on Jesus in the midst of pain and suffering.

> *When peace like a river attendeth my way,*
> *When sorrow like sea billows roll,*
> *Whatever my lot, thou has caused me to say*
> *It is well, it is well with my soul.*

I have sung this song more times than I can count in my life. However, it was not until I was pastoring Center City Church and I chose to teach on the topic of lament that I explored the backstory of the song. Upon learning the devastating motivation of the song, I began to embrace it in seasons of loss, pain, and despair in a new way.

My friend Mack Brock recently wrote a song that pulled from elements of this classic hymn called "Still in Control." I'm so grateful that Mack chose to enter into a season of lament so that he could pen a song for a new generation of believers. We need more songs like these in our churches today. We need to learn to lament in a way that fixes our attention on God and resonates deeply with the real experiences of people who fill our churches on any given Sunday. If you are a pastor, will you have the courage to lead your congregation into seasons of lament that will teach them how to properly grieve the ills of the culture that surrounds us? Or will you choose to only sing songs of celebration that force your congregation to figure out on their own how to properly grieve the pain they experience in the real world?

We must do a better job in the current context of our church communities to help people recognize, name, and appropriately respond to their pain. Additionally, we need to learn what it means to lament with groups of people who are hurting and experiencing deep feelings of grief and loss.

Immigrant families are mourning the loss of family members being ripped away from their homes and deported back to their home countries, leaving children motherless and fatherless in neighborhoods in our cities.

Native American families grieve the fact that entire cities have been developed on land that was originally owned by their ancestors. Instead of being compensated and negotiating a fair price for the land, thousands of Native Americans were forcibly removed from their rightful land and sent across the country to reservations that were unfamiliar.

Every time a black man is a victim of a police-related death, the community laments. The senseless death of another young man is a loss for everyone, not just his immediate family.

Until white people choose to listen, learn, and grow regarding matters of race and economics, we will continue to enjoy a system that benefits us while our neighbors of color lament. We will not lament until we allow ourselves to feel pain, and we will not feel pain until we choose to learn about the experience of our neighbors.

When we listen to the cries of our neighbors we will learn to grieve together. As we grieve together, we can build friendships with people who are different from us. When we build friendships with people that are different than us, we will be moved to tears when we hear of the news of Eric, Michael, Tamir, Freddie, Alton, Philando, Rodney, Keith, and so many others that are being impacted by unjust and unequal systems in our culture.

We can't look away. No matter how heartbreaking or uncomfortable.

We have looked away far too long.

We can't look away.

Open your eyes and your heart.

Care. Weep. Lament.

Our brothers and sisters are dying.

In order to experience true healing, we must learn to lament with our neighbors.

***

Throughout each round of editing this chapter, at least three of our brothers and one of our sisters were killed in law-enforcement related incidents. Protests filled the streets as we made final edits and sent this book to the printer.

No justice, no peace.

An ocean of lament. A sea of sadness.

God, please help us to open our eyes and our hearts to see and feel the pain of our neighbors.

Ahmaud Arbery was killed on February 23, 2020 in Brunswick, GA. Breonna Taylor was killed on March 13, 2020 in Louisville, KY. George Floyd was killed on May 25, 2020 in Minneapolis, MN. Rayshard Brooks was killed on June 12, 2020 in Atlanta, GA.

My heart is heavy, but my hope is in Jesus.

We Belong to One Another

Jesus Christ is the neighbor to all of us.
—Amos Yong, *Hospitality and the Other*

"Why don't any of *them* ever come to these meetings?"

I thought my heart was going to beat out of my chest. A group of forty leaders from local government, churches, nonprofit organizations, and businesses had gathered at my invitation to discuss gentrification and inequality.

Robert is the pastor of a predominantly white and well-known church in the Charlotte community. "Look around the room," he continued. "Every time I come to one of these meetings, your friends from minority communities never attend. I want to know why."

His tone was demeaning and demanding.

The silence in the room was blaring in my ears.

Everyone turned to look at me to see how I would respond.

"Robert," I said, speaking slower than normal and reminding myself to breathe, "if you grew up with inequality all around and familiar neighborhoods were redeveloped against your will over and over again, would you show up to a lesson on that experience? My friends have lived this lesson."

He stared back at me with a smug half-smile on his face.

"Also," I continued, "can we move away from saying things like *those people* and *them* about my friends? We are all connected. We came here today because all of us in this room have some learning to do before we will ever understand the experiences of our neighbors."

Robert stood up at the conclusion of the meeting and immediately headed for the exit. He left without saying a word to me or anyone else. However, Alvin made a direct line toward me. I didn't know Alvin well at the time, but he wanted to thank me for saying what I said to Robert.

"I really hesitated to accept the invitation to this meeting," he said. "I am normally looked at to speak for all black people. That is not what I want to do all the time. When you spoke up today, it meant a lot to me, and I just want to thank you. Someone needed to say what you said. I am excited to see how we can partner together for the sake of our city moving forward."

We are one family, created in the beautiful image of God (Genesis 1:27). We need to move away from statements that create an *us* versus *them* scenario. As image-bearers of the same Father, each one of us reflects a different aspect of the beauty of God. When we separate ourselves from others who are different from us, we cannot see the fullness of the beauty of God.

***

"Thanks for joining us on Delta Airlines. We hope your flight is a pleasant one."

The captain flawlessly delivered his well-rehearsed greeting as if everything was normal. But nothing was normal about this particular flight. I grew up on planes. My dad retired from Delta Airlines after a thirty-year career with the company. Many of my childhood memories include whimsical, last-minute trips to destinations that fascinated my mom. Traveling is in our blood. Because of this, I am somewhat immune to the preflight script from the captain and flight attendants. I know how to buckle my seat belt and how to put the air mask on myself before the person next to me in the unlikely event of an emergency. However, I was paying much closer attention this time.

The woman directly in front of my seat spent five minutes deep-cleaning her entire row with disinfectant wipes. I had intended to do the same, but when I went to get the wipes I purchased to clean my area, I was shocked to see that I had purchased individual packs of Shout wipes. I'm not sure that a pandemic can be staved off by stain-removing wipes.

COVID-19—the coronavirus—was a bit of a mystery to many of us on the half-full plane that evening. My friend, Doug, and I boarded the red-eye flight to London for a six-day ministry trip. We had heard news of a virus that was rapidly impacting the globe, but Charlotte and London were yet to be impacted on a large scale . . . Or so I thought. Little did I know that the virus was very much at home and in London.

During my online research while preparing for the trip, I learned that I should clean my arm rests and tray tables. One internet site said that the tray table has more germs than the toilet seat on a plane because people sneeze directly onto the surface located approximately three feet from their face. Made sense to me.

Luckily, I found some hand sanitizer and I used a napkin to scrub my area clean.

As I settled in for the overnight flight, I was pleased to see that no one was sitting next to me. I like people, but not so much when their knee is touching mine on an eight-hour flight. My intention was to enjoy a few hours of writing and then try to get a good night of rest. I use the term "good night of rest" loosely when talking about trying to sleep on a plane.

I took out my computer and placed it on the extremely clean tray table in front of my seat. The moment I connected to Wi-Fi, I discovered that the world was starting to shut down. A headline flashed across the screen stating that travel from Europe to America had been banned. After a few hours of uncertainty, Doug and I were assured that we would be able to return home.

As we prepared to land, I looked out the window, down on a world in turmoil. I didn't know how the world would be different when the plane landed or in the weeks and months to come. The more I researched, the more my heart broke for all the people whose lives would be deeply affected by this pandemic—people who would lose their lives, lose family members, lose jobs, lose financial stability, lose childcare, and so much more.

When the plane landed, my heart was heavy as I struggled to come to terms with the new reality we were now living in. I was on a return flight within twenty-five hours. I continued thinking about my friends in West Charlotte and the devastating impact the virus and the pandemic would have on the community.

***

Jesus made a habit of agitating the religious leaders of the day. Not so much because He was intentionally trying to upset them, but because He did not care about their man-made rules that created unnecessary and ungodly separation between people who were different from one another. He expected the same of those who chose to follow Him.

He expects the same of us.

Upon finishing a long day of ministry, Jesus found Himself in a private moment with His closest disciples on a hillside. One of the men asked Jesus to discuss the signs that will point to His return. Instead of answering his question directly, Jesus embarked on a wide-ranging teaching. The Mount of Olives provided a beautiful backdrop of rolling hills and the brilliance of nature as He took His disciples on a journey.

Jesus describes His second coming to the earth in Matthew 25:31–46. He describes a majestic scene where unnamed and unnumbered amounts of angels join Him as He sits upon a glorious throne.

And then He talks about neighborliness.

Jesus said there are some who will be on His right and

some on His left. The ones on His right chose to embody the message of Jesus during their time on the earth. The ones on His left chose their own path. To the ones on the right, Jesus describes a beautiful scene in which those who embodied His love did so by the way they treated their neighbors when they were in need. He said, "For I was hungry, and you fed me. I was thirsty, and you gave me a drink. I was a stranger, and you invited me into your home. I was naked, and you gave me clothing. I was sick, and you cared for me. I was in prison, and you visited me" (Mathew 25:35–36).

Continuing with their ever-so-literal interpretation of the teaching of Jesus, the disciples responded with confusion, "When did we ever do this for you?"

"I tell you the truth," Jesus replied, "when you did it to one of the least of these my brothers and sisters, you were doing it to me!" (v. 40).

The Savior of the world is saying that when I reach out to my neighbors in need, I am reaching out to Jesus Himself. Jesus is present with those who are overlooked, pushed aside, and marginalized in our culture.

Then Jesus described the ones who were gathered on His left. They are the ones who chose their own path and did not embody His love for the sake of their neighbors. He looked to them and said, "I tell you the truth, when you refused to help the least of these my brothers and sisters, you were refusing to help me" (v. 45).

My brothers and sisters.

Not only does Jesus paint a picture of His presence with those that are hurting, He self-identifies as their sibling. The closeness and tenderness of Jesus toward those who are often cast aside is absolutely stunning and inspiring. I want to embody this same love for my neighbors when they are in need.

The general public's response to COVID-19 illuminated this teaching of Jesus' in a new way for me. I saw a two-fold effect: first, humanity's instinct to care for one another was on display; second, corrupt social systems were clearly exposed. I saw people feed the hungry, provide shelter for the homeless, and care for the sick, and I saw corrupt systems take advantage of the marginalized, employers treat their employees unfairly, and wealth and privilege be the determining factor between life and death.

***

"Wow!" The email from the executive director at Urban-Promise Charlotte read. "In the span of twenty-four hours, you all have donated enough money to allow us to purchase $50 gift cards for every single family we serve—all 350 families."

UrbanPromise Charlotte is the after-school program for kids in West Charlotte that is hosted at Center City Church. The outbreak of COVID-19 forced programming to be immediately shut down in all three of their Charlotte locations. Many of the students and their families were left uncertain about what steps to take next. Generous donors in the Charlotte community raised $17,500 in less than a day to help make sure there was some immediate relief for families as they were trying to navigate this new reality. The generosity did not holistically fix the problem, but I believe that every dollar donated in that moment of crisis was donated as unto the Lord. UrbanPromise is not only the best after-school program I've seen, but also the best discipleship program. Their vision is threefold: reach a child, raise a leader, and restore a community.[29] They accomplish this by employing high school students as counselors, tutors, and mentors for elementary and middle school-aged children who attend after-school programs and summer camps.

The children arrive at UrbanPromise at 3:05 p.m. and rumble through the lobby of Center City Church and into the multipurpose room. They are given snacks and drinks and then split up into their classes. StreetLeaders—the high schoolers employed by UrbanPromise—help them complete their homework, counsel them if they have had a hard day, and then enjoy dinner together before being picked up by family or friends at 6:00 p.m.

When UrbanPromise had to unexpectedly shut down their daily operation, the harsh reality of poverty was clearly exposed. Many of the StreetLeaders work as a way to help their families make ends meet each month. If they are not able to work, utility bills may not be paid. Rent may become overdue. Furthermore, the StreetLeaders are given drinks and snacks before they start their shift and they enjoy dinner with the kids after the program is done each day—one less meal they have to provide for themselves.

No UrbanPromise means less money and less food.

No UrbanPromise means uncertainty for the children and their families. The parents have to deal with new realities and answer seemingly unsolvable questions, such as: How can I still work if I cannot send my children to UrbanPromise after school? If I cannot work, how will I pay my rent on time? If I cannot work, how will I feed my babies?

These are just a few of the questions that devastated the families at UrbanPromise in the disruptive wake of COVID-19.

Families in middle, upper-middle, and upper-class economic communities in Charlotte were disrupted as well. Everyone was impacted with this historic pandemic. However, those who could least afford to have their lives interrupted were impacted the most. While the pandemic was inconvenient for most people in middle, upper-middle, and upper-class economic communities, it directly impacted the well-being and livelihood of those who live in high-poverty communities.

COVID-19 highlighted the underlying realities that were already present in every high-poverty community across our country. Hard-working parents living paycheck-to-paycheck were given no choice but to stay home with their children at the expense of their jobs. No matter how hard families worked, the reality was that many still needed the help of others. The helping networks within these communities were affected by the stay-at-home orders, which made making ends meet a lot harder for countless families.

Every person was challenged in the new reality of the world. Those blessed with financial resources were challenged to share like never before. Those who needed financial resources were challenged to humbly reach out and let others know their needs.

No one asked for a pandemic, but we learned so much by living through the experience. In many ways, we learned how to *see* each other again. Systemic inequities overlooked in the normal news cycles were now headline news every day.

Kids who relied on lunch at school as their only meal of the day could no longer rely on that meal. Families without access to Wi-Fi or the technology needed for online education had to figure how they could finish the school year. Grocery store workers now considered essential had to keep working to make ends meet but, in doing so, risked their health. Single parents who needed to work to pay the bills now had to find a way to pay for childcare. Part-time and hourly workers were laid off in record-setting numbers. Two and a half million people filed for unemployment benefits during the first week of the pandemic clearly hitting America. People started to plainly see that some had "pandemic-proof" jobs and others who didn't and who lived paycheck to paycheck were adversely affected by this new reality. The pandemic did not create economic imbalance in our communities, the pandemic exposed economic imbalance in our communities.

I personally witnessed the absolute breathtaking joy of Christ-like generosity from those who viewed their finances through the lens of neighborliness. Conversely, I saw the devastation of others who did not have the social capital to reach out in their time of need. Robert Putnam says, "Social scientists often use the term *social capital* to describe social connectedness—that is ties to family, friends, neighbors and acquaintances; involvement in civic associations, religious institutions, athletic teams, volunteer activities; and so on."[30]

The pandemic clearly exposed our need for neighborliness in our communities. We have needed one another all along, but the security of a strong economy and record-setting profits lead many to believe they are self-sufficient. However, the pandemic has exposed the connection that we all have to one another. My actions directly impact the actions of others.

As weeks turned into months of staying at home, millions of people around the world were experiencing the fact that their actions directly impacted the health and livelihood of others in their community. My prayer is that we will take the lessons learned during the pandemic and make the connection to our lives outside of a unique season of awareness. I pray we would understand the connectedness we have to our neighbors. I pray we choose to love people, welcome them into our world, and use our voice to highlight the brilliance of others that may be pushed aside, overlooked, and marginalized.

Jacques Ellul said, "When we see someone as our neighbor, we see a person to whom we are responsible."[31] We feed the hungry, we speak for the voiceless, we care for the sick, because when we do so, we care for our brothers and sisters and we represent the love of Jesus.

We belong to one another.

8

Toxic Charity

The church needs to develop cultural intelligence in
order to fully realize the many-colored tapestry that
God is weaving together.
—**Soong-Chan Rah,** *Many Colors*

"It doesn't feel good to me," Roman said as we were enjoying catching up at our go-to local coffee shop.

"What's that?" I asked my friend.

"When churches come to high-poverty communities to volunteer *en masse* for a week at a time, and we have to find things for them to do because they are some of our biggest supporters and it is part of our funding agreement."

Roman lowered his voice as he looked down at his cappuccino, "David, I don't know how to tell them that their efforts are distracting us from the work we are trying to do around here. Finding unnecessary work for volunteers is more of a burden to us than they realize."

My heart hurt for my friend.

"It's part of the game, though," he said. "They are going to present a $50,000 check when they come today. If we don't have that check, we won't be able to make it to the end of the year."

"Tell me more," I said. "I genuinely want to learn from your experience."

"Here's the biggest problem," Roman said, still talking a few decibels lower than normal. "When a bunch of people from the suburbs show up over the course of the week, all of the kids we are working with get really excited. There's nothing particularly bad about what happens through the week. The volunteers are genuinely having a blast with the kids."

Roman paused as he played with the foam in his half-full drink.

"However, the kids get attached, David. When those same volunteers don't show up for another year, it perpetuates the feeling in high-poverty communities that people do not come for relationships. They come to check off a volunteer box. The kids miss their new friends, and we are left to clean up the pieces."

***

We were sitting at the kitchen table in our home when Marcus and Carrie—missionaries in South America—explained to Dara and me that short-term trips overseas can be more of a burden than a help. My perspective changed when I realized that churches in first-world countries offer help that is often not valuable to missionaries who live in these communities permanently. "Some of the trips are very beneficial to us and our community. However, some are not and we feel compelled to host short-term groups because of the support that comes the rest of the year from those churches," Carrie admitted. "But it can be exhausting."

As a pastor, I have been both on the offering end of unwanted help and the receiving end. Being on the receiving end of unwanted help made me significantly more aware and sensitive to how damaging outside, temporary help can be for communities trying to create systemic change. On the surface, volunteering seems like a good thing, right? However, volunteerism that is not rooted in relationship and understanding can be toxic.

***

"Hi, thanks for coming today! Are you here to volunteer?" A man in a brightly colored volunteer shirt welcomed me to the lobby of the church.

"Hi," I replied with a bit of confusion. "No, I am one of the pastors here. My name is David. Who are you?"

"Oh hey, so great to meet you, pastor David. Thanks for hosting us. My name is Todd, and we are here to volunteer for the week," he replied.

"Volunteer for what?" I asked, completely confused at this point.

"The summer camp," Todd replied.

"You mean the summer camp we run for kids in downtown Orlando?" I asked.

"Yes. We are fifty strong today. We have ice cream for the kids, and the entire team has prepared games to play with the kids."

Just then, I saw the camp director, Michael, walking briskly down the hall.

"Nice to meet you," I said to Todd as I jogged to catch up to Michael.

"Michael," I asked, "what's going on here?"

The previous evening, Michael received a phone call from the camp's biggest donor—a large, local church. Michael did not feel as if he could say no when the outreach pastor called and said she was trying to find a spot for fifty more volunteers for the church's outreach week. So the next day, those fifty volunteers showed up to serve as a part of the coordinated week of serving across the city.

Michael's original plan for the week was to get the kids started on a reading program that would be interactive, fun, and helpful for the kids. The goal was to help the kids continue improving their reading over the summer instead of declining. He wanted to help them prepare for the upcoming school year and equip them to succeed in their education. The staff had been working on this reading initiative all week. However, the night before camp started, Michael got the request from the church to accommodate fifty volunteers. His heart broke as he said yes to the large church's request.

"Pastor David," he whispered in the hallway, "we only give ice cream to the kids on Fridays as a treat for their hard work. It's 10:00 a.m. on Monday. The kids are going to go crazy on a sugar rush. Our programming is completely interrupted because of this."

No one asked Michael if fifty volunteers would be helpful that week. No one asked me (or anyone else) if a large group of people could set up their ice cream party and games in the lobby of our church. No one took the time to consider what was best for the kids that day. The large church needed to fill volunteer slots, and the summer camp was the perfect place to send them at the last minute.

The kids had a blast. They ate ice cream and played games with the adults in the colorful shirts while the paid staff at the summer camp watched in confusion. They were supposed to be running the planned program for the week. But instead, fifty people were there playing with kids they didn't know and most likely would never see again.

At the end of the day, I called the executive pastor at the large church.

"Lisa, what was that about today?" I asked, trying to hold back my frustration.

"Hey," Lisa replied. "I'm so sorry no one called you, but I heard the event went really well. I heard the kids were really into the ice cream and games."

My heart started to race. "Lisa," I said, "Your team showed up on less than twenty-four hours' notice and left a huge mess. I have a service in here tonight and the trash cans are overflowing with ice cream boxes, bowls, and supplies from the games. Our parking lot has trash everywhere."

"Are you really going to focus on the mess that was made during that event instead of the impact that was made yesterday?" Lisa replied dismissively. "We are trying to co-ordinate over 15,000 hours of volunteer service this week at sites across the city. I hope we can celebrate a team win today instead of being frustrated about a bit of a mess."

"A team win," I replied, "means that everyone wins. Did

the team win when the camp staff had to change their programming to accommodate your last-minute request? Did the team win when the kids had their schedules disrupted to have a blast with fifty strangers? Did the team win when my staff spent the day cleaning instead of preparing for the service tonight?"

I could sense that my point was not landing.

"I just wish that you guys would consider what's best for the people you say that you are serving when you plan these events," I said. "Please, let's try to coordinate in the future."

"I'm sorry you're upset, David," Lisa replied. "But a lot of good was done in the city today. We'll try to do better next time."

* * *

Serving our communities can oftentimes be misguided and unhelpful to the very people we want to serve. What the kids really needed that Monday morning in Orlando was to start working toward their goal of improving their reading scores. They needed a rhythm and routine to settle into, which would include fun and snacks. But first, they needed to read. And the staff had worked diligently to strike a balance between working hard and having a blast.

Bob Lupton wrote a book that explored this type of scenario called *Toxic Charity: How Churches and Charities Hurt Those They Help, And How to Reverse It.*[32] The premise of the book is that many well-intentioned people and churches send people into high-poverty communities genuinely wanting to help. However, many times the end result is actually a net negative outcome for the neighborhood. When speaking with Bob about these ideas, he said, "Healthy relationships are always reciprocal. Those of us who have access to resources are charged to design systems with reciprocity in mind. No one likes to be anybody's charity case."

Reciprocity, in this case, would mean that Lisa and Michael would work together to find a solution that met both of their needs. There is nothing wrong with a week full of serving communities. Unless, of course, a goal of 15,000 hours of service is more important than the people supposedly being served.

Toxic charity led Lisa to surprise Michael with fifty volunteers who brought confusion and distraction to the summer camp. The reason Todd did not know he was hurting more than helping was because neither he nor Lisa asked Michael how they could be most helpful. And that is the problem with many suburban churches that are trying to do outreach programs in lower income communities.

We need less outreach and more relationships.

We need more holistic understanding of one another rather than exciting weeks of service.

We need to *see* each other.

If Lisa would have called Michael the night before and explained the situation to him, he may have been able to break up the group of fifty into smaller groups to serve in a way that would have been genuinely helpful. After-school programs and summer camps for kids are successful because they have leaders who are creative and courageous. Adapting on the fly is the name of the game. However, in this scenario, Lisa positioned herself as the expert in the room and Michael was the means to an end. She was tasked with the responsibility of getting volunteer hours covered. As she stated, the goal of the church was to accomplish 15,000 of volunteer hours in one week.

If you lead a church or an organization that has done weeks of service for your city, I am not writing this with a judgmental spirit. I have been where you are and I have made well-intentioned mistakes. I do not believe your heart is in a bad place or that you are intentionally trying to be self-serving for your organization. However, I have seen the other side of these type of activities. I have made friends who honestly share their experiences with me. If outreach to our neighbors is not rooted in relationship, we will never be able to truly assess what is needed. Toxic charity does not lead to or promote genuine relationships.

I acknowledge that most people are genuinely motivated by their faith to help others in need. Here are some ideas and questions to help you consider your steps forward.

- Instead of calling neighborhood organizations or nonprofits to tell them what you want to do for them, could you call and ask if they need or want help?
- If they do need help, ask them how many volunteers would be needed and what specific tasks would be ideal to be accomplished.
- Ask them if your presence will be helpful accomplishing the mission of their organization.

- If you are financially supporting a nonprofit organization through your church, business, or personal philanthropy, would you consider *not* tying stipulations of volunteer opportunities to the organization unless they specifically ask for help? The organizations need your donations, but they oftentimes do not need an immense amount of volunteer help at one time.

***

To this day, I still don't make all the right calls. I have a heart to love, serve, and genuinely be a blessing to others. But I need to continually check my heart and my motives and be open to honest feedback from the people in my community.

"David," my friend Sam said to me, "your heart is in the right place. I know you want to help a lot of people. But what I really want for you is to simply go deep with one organization. Pick one place and just settle into the relationships that are formed in that one place. Make sure you know people's names and they know yours. This is my biggest desire for you."

Sam has been a consistent presence in my life for almost ten years. He speaks truth in love. He longs for me to continue digging deep into my passion for helping families in poverty. He also knows that the way to truly make a difference is to build relationships and be impacted by relationships with my neighbors.

When you have a relationship with someone living in poverty, the issues are no longer far away. The systemic inequality that is present in our society is no longer a point to be debated or a volunteer box to check off. When you build relationships, you fight *for* friends who are hurting.

When we push our own agenda in regard to helping others, our service is self-serving and can be damaging to communities that are trying to build systemic change and mitigate the hardships of those in need. When we humbly listen to what is needed from those actively and permanently serving their community and help fight for those things, our service ceases to be self-serving and becomes beneficial for long-term community development. Solutions for families to disrupt the pattern of poverty are most effective when they come from neighbors within their own community. After all, no one knows a neighborhood better than the family who has lived there for generations. Instead of showing up with answers, let's learn to ask better questions.

When service is rooted in relationship, everyone participates in a meaningful way.

9

Everyone Participates

We have to allow ourselves—our beliefs and actions—
to be shaped into instruments for love and justice.
We cannot solve the problem of being divided
by being divided.
—**Dr. Lucretia Berry**, *What Lies Between Us*

"David, what would you do if you had a significant amount of money to reach the West Charlotte community?"

I was in an executive board room filled with five wealthy, well-known, and influential businessmen. They had been gathering for three months to explore the Bible, pray, and discuss what they might be able to do to bring healing and equity to high-poverty communities in Charlotte.

"I would give it to Joel," I replied.

"Excuse me?" one of the men replied. Each of them curiously looked at me, then each other, then back at me again.

"Joel has been in the neighborhood for over fifteen years doing great work. If I had a significant amount of money to reach the West Charlotte community, I would give it to someone that has a proven track record. I would give it to Joel."

***

Center City Church had been in the West Charlotte neighborhood for six months when I was invited to attend a meeting at an office complex in South Charlotte. The invitation came from a mutual friend in the nonprofit community who was helping this group of men navigate their desire to use their resources for the benefit of their neighbors.

Upon receiving the invitation to join them for a meeting regarding the potential to fund a significant work in West Charlotte, I prayed that God would help me to have proper motives for agreeing to attend. I did not want to be swayed by the opportunity to join a well-funded effort just because it was well funded.

I hadn't been in the neighborhood long, but I was immersed in my doctoral studies exploring the cyclical patterns of generational poverty. One report after another told the stories of multimillion-dollar efforts that resulted in little to no measurable impact in high-poverty communities across the country.

There seemed to be no shortage of wealthy business owners and corporations that wanted to make a difference in their community. However, the missing piece between highly motivated businesspeople and the ability to achieve sustainable and measurable change seemed to be a willingness to patiently explore best practices from places that have seen sustainable change occur in their neighborhoods.

Admittedly, I did not have a clue how to make a meaningful impact in West Charlotte. I told them to fund someone who had a sustained history of meaningful and effective work in the community. Joel had been supporting education programs for kids in West Charlotte for fifteen years. The relationships he had formed with students, families, teachers, and administrators was inspiring and impressive.

The five men around the table asked great questions that led to a robust conversation over the course of ninety minutes. I thanked them for their time and excused myself, never expecting to hear back from them after such an unconventional funding meeting.

I found out a few weeks later that one of the men in the room gave Joel $10,000.

God Defends the Poor

The Scriptures are full of stories about God's heart for the poor.

Does this mean that God shows favoritism to those who are in poverty over those who are wealthy? I have always believed that God is not biased toward the poor; He loves every person equally, no matter their financial status. But He will fiercely defend those that are oppressed, overlooked, and marginalized.

Ronald Sider wrote a book that addressed this topic called *Rich Christians in an Age of Hunger.* He said,

> God, however, is not neutral. His freedom from bias does not mean that he maintains neutrality in the struggle for justice.

The Bible clearly and repeatedly teaches that God is at work in
history exalting the poor and casting down the rich who got
that way by oppressing or neglecting the poor. In that sense,
God is on the side of the poor. He has a special concern for
them because of their vulnerability.[33]

Christians should have an informed understanding of
economic systems and structures because they are regularly discussed throughout the Old and New Testaments. Unjust economic systems are clearly and repeatedly rebuked.
Equitable and fair treatment of all neighbors is praised and
counted as godly and beautiful.

Understanding how culture has been formed and continues to be organized is just as important now as it was
then. We cannot discern how to love our neighbors well if
we do not understand the way in which the world operates.
We must understand that we are all on the same playing
field, but the rules of the game are not always equal for
everyone involved.

If the desire for wealth, influence, and power supersedes
the message of generous love for others, the gospel message
has been distorted and perverted in favor of a system that
views a group of perceived *haves* over a group of perceived
have nots.

This is not the gospel.

The book of Proverbs supports the cause of the poor by
revealing God's heart for those who have been marginalized and cast aside from the dominant culture of excess and
greed. Proverbs 14:31 says, "Those who oppress the poor
insult their Maker, but helping the poor honors him." Prov-

erbs 19:17 states, "If you help the poor, you are lending to the LORD—and he will repay you!" The form of repayment is not always found in financial gain. Conversely, it is rare that helping someone in need would naturally increase an individual's net wealth. However, the implication of God's heart for the poor is that the blessings of God will be upon those who turn their attention to the poor and work toward their benefit.

Individuals who experience a measure of wealth have a unique opportunity to embody the message of Jesus that is defined by generosity, joy, and open-handed care for others. I do not believe it is a sin to be wealthy. However, the pursuit of God should always and forever supersede the pursuit of wealth.

Jesus had access to all power and authority, yet He willingly poured Himself out for the benefit of others. He expects the same of each one of us.

Philippians 2:5–11 states:

> You must have the same attitude that Christ Jesus had. Though he was God, he did not think of equality with God as something to cling to. Instead, he gave up his divine privileges; he took the humble position of a slave and was born as a human being. When he appeared in human form, he humbled himself in obedience to God and died a criminal's death on a cross. Therefore, God elevated him to the place of highest honor and gave him the name above all other names. That at the name of Jesus every knee should bow, in heaven and on earth and under the earth, and every tongue declare that Jesus Christ is Lord, to the glory of God the Father.

Jesus chose to abstain from the full expression of His power so that the power of God could be on display. There is no amount of earthly power, influence, wealth, or authority that will ever break the bondage of poverty. Bryan Stevenson, social justice activist, lawyer, and author of *Just Mercy*, said, "My work with the poor and the incarcerated has persuaded me that the opposite of poverty is not wealth; the opposite of poverty is justice."[34] We must pray that the Lord guides and directs our resources in order to experience restoration, justice, and healing that is beyond what any one person or corporation can afford.

Sustainable and meaningful change will come when genuine relationships between the rich and the poor begin to form. All too often, however, people who have experienced a measure of wealth believe that their resources and ideas are what will bring change to a community. A lack of patience causes many well-meaning people not to take the proper amount of time to listen, learn, and holistically work with longtime residents. The end result is largely not what anyone longed for at the outset of the work.

The Bible does not say that the resources of the wealthy will defend the poor. God Himself defends the poor. Jesus seemed to embody the plight of people living in poverty as He told His disciples that any time they gave to the poor, they were actually giving to Jesus Himself (Matthew 25:31–46). He consistently enjoyed genuine relationships with those that were pushed to the margins. This does not sound like the behavior of a distant deity that is aloof or disconnected to the cries of the poor. God Himself is present with the poor, and if Christians want to be present with their Creator, they can find Him among the weak and marginalized. Let's join Him in His work.

***

I couldn't believe my eyes when I got another invitation to meet with the aforementioned group of businessmen. We had another very good meeting. I was beginning to believe that these men were genuinely seeking the Lord and trying to find a way to make a real and meaningful investment into the Charlotte community.

I was invited back a total of five times over the course of four months to discuss my doctoral studies and the practical things I was learning by our church's presence in West Charlotte. Each meeting concluded similarly. I was asked what could be accomplished if a significant amount of money was available to invest into the West Charlotte community.

Each time, I deflected the question.

Honestly, part of my hesitation was that I did not know these men well. I was exposed to some exciting research, and my mind was going a million miles an hour. I had practical ideas, but I had yet to share them because I was building trust with a new group of friends. I knew they were growing tired of discussing the issues with seemingly no forward movement, but I figured it was better never to receive an invitation back into that room than to move too quickly and cause more harm in our well-intentioned efforts to bring change to West Charlotte.

I was walking down the middle of the ninth fairway

at Myers Park Country Club with one of the businessmen when he finally reached a point of exasperation.

"David," he said, "we have been talking with you over the course of the last four months and you haven't shared any practical ideas with us. We have had great conversations, but we genuinely want to help."

"I am getting to know you guys," I replied. "I have seen too many well-intentioned businesspeople try to go into high-poverty communities and cause more harm than good. I am not trying to be offensive. I just want to be measured in the way we explore potentially working together."

"I totally get that," he responded. "We just want to hear some ideas. We want to do our part in seeing real and meaningful change come to our city."

"Ok," I relented. "Let's talk then."

He stared back at me with a look of shock and intrigue.

"I think you guys should pause," I said. He cocked his head to the left a bit, and I could see the disappointment in his eyes. "Hang on," I continued. "Pausing does not equal doing nothing. Just like with any business venture, you need to plan where you are going before you embark on the journey. Education *is* action."

He agreed.

I continued, "Take six months and research various nonprofits, churches, and organizations that actually show results for what you are hoping to accomplish. Hire someone to explore communities that have seen measurable and sustained change over the course of a long period of time."

To my surprise, he was still nodding in agreement.

"Your money will be better spent if it is supported by

prayer, patience, and research. I think you and your friends should consider funding an effort to send someone all over the country to talk to organizations and community-led initiatives that have made a measurable difference in high-poverty communities."

I am not sure what I was expecting, but his look of genuine curiosity and openness struck me as sincere. Sensing a real moment to share what had been on my heart for months, I finally spoke openly.

"One of the things I have seen with wealthy business-people is that they are used to getting things done their way," I said as I stared directly in his eyes. "I need you to know that this community will never say yes to this group because of your money. I know you guys want to help, but you need to be ready for resistance. You will simply be viewed as another group of wealthy white guys bringing new development and initiatives into a predominantly black community. It will take time to build trust."

I was almost positive that was the end of the conversation.

He immediately replied, "That sounds great!"

It does? I thought to myself while trying to keep a straight face.

He looked at me squarely in the eyes, "Will you do it?"

"Yes," I responded before I even fully knew what happened.

The Body of Christ

Approximately sixty years after the life, death, and resurrection of Jesus, the gospel message had spread like wildfire across Asia Minor. It was an exciting time for this early band of believers. However, a dangerous tension was unfolding.

The perfect message of Jesus had been left in the imperfect hands of God's most beloved creation. Normal people like you and me were the ones who would pass the beautiful message of salvation, joy, and freedom that comes through relationship with Jesus.

The apostle Paul wrote a letter to a group of believers who lived in a vibrant city center called Ephesus. Think of New York City, Paris, or London. As a thriving commerce center, this community was also a melting pot for many religions, ethnicities, and a broad array of socio-economic statuses. Paul established a church in a world-class city, and the church was expanding rapidly.

However, the fast-growing early church seemed to be making some missteps along the way. Paul wrote a beautiful letter in the New Testament called *Ephesians*. His intention was to reestablish best practices for the early church and to give clear teaching on what it meant to be a unique community of Christ followers.

"Please don't call them Christ followers, David."

I can hear my professor, Dr. Len Sweet, in my head right now. "We are not called to follow Jesus. We are called to embody His love for this world." With that being said, Paul wanted to teach believers what it meant to be a unique community of *Christ embodiers*. Paul was encouraging the Ephesian believers to literally take on the characteristics of Christ by showing His love to others through their actions.

Ephesians 4:11–16 clearly lays out the plan of God to redeem a broken and hurting world. The prevailing metaphor of the church is found in this passage. The body of Christ has many parts, each with a unique and vital purpose. Paul says there are gifts given to the body of Christ—apostles, prophets, evangelists, shepherds, and teachers. The idea here is that we are all wired differently, but uniquely called to do our part. This was and is God's plan for His Church.

Everyone participates.

Our current church culture needs an awakening. We need to clearly understand that *all* believers have been called to fulfill the greatest commandment of loving God and neighbors. The plan was not for one charismatic leader to know and be known by God and then tell everyone what to do. The plan of God was to know and be known by everyone. Neil Cole in his book *Church 3.0* said, "Sound leadership in a movement is not coming up with the vision and then casting it to others, but instead helping others find a vision for themselves and releasing it to the ends of the earth."[35]

The greatest aim of the Church is not to grow the local church. Jesus said that our job was to learn how to cast aside distractions and love Him with every part of our heart, mind, soul, and strength. Additionally, He said that it was of utmost importance that we learned how to love one another in the same way we love ourselves. Instead of fumbling our way through church mission statements and new vision initiatives, we could do this a lot more simply. We could look at what Jesus clearly told us was the most important thing, and do it.

Paul encourages the believers in Ephesus to be unified: different parts, one body. How do we even begin to pursue unity when our culture has deep dividing lines seared into its very fabric? Part of crossing dividing lines is celebrating differences. "If the whole body were an eye, how would you hear? Or if your whole body were an ear, how would you smell anything? But our bodies have many parts, and God has put each part just where he wants it" (1 Corinthians 12:17–18). When we celebrate our differences, we embolden everyone to participate.

In order to actively celebrate our differences, everyone needs to do their part to look inward. We need to do the heartbreaking and emotional work of learning each other's stories in order to fulfill the most important command that Jesus gave us. Additionally, God has given each one of us gifts that can be used to bring equality to our communities.

In other words, everyone participates.

* * *

I have always believed that vision is like a puzzle. At the beginning, there are pieces scattered everywhere. I can put a bunch of pieces down to get the puzzle going, but inevitably I get stuck along the way. Someone else can come along and see the puzzle from a different perspective and put one piece down that unlocks ten more pieces.

The creation of Freedom Communities has been like a puzzle. This is the organization that came out of the time I spent with the business leaders who wanted to make a meaningful investment into our community.

During the formative stages of this organization, I could see a basic framework forming in my mind, but I needed a group of like-minded business and nonprofit leaders to unlock the other pieces. I knew that research was going to be important to build the foundation of our work, but I could not get there alone. The participation of the residents in West Charlotte, the business leaders that wanted to make a meaningful investment in their community, and nonprofit leaders who would partner with us was absolutely vital.

We needed everyone to participate.

However, before we started the organization, we needed a season of humbly listening, learning, and growing. The group of business leaders who initially invited me to speak at their gathering committed to invest financially into a season of research and travel. This was a dream come true for Dara and me. Through their generosity, we were going to be able to get boots on the ground in communities that we had studied from a distance. We were ecstatic.

Over the next four months, we had the privilege of visiting several holistic community development organizations: Lawndale Christian Health Center in Chicago, Purpose Built Communities in Atlanta, DC Dream Center in Washington, DC, and a gathering of practitioners in Detroit at the Christian Community Developers Association Conference. We began to realize that every place we visited had a holistic view of community development. There was not one program or organization that led to sustainable change, but many people were coming together for the benefit of their neighbors.

Our trip to Chicago showed us what could happen if we focused on one geographic location over a long period of time. Wayne Gordon and John Perkins committed to the

North Lawndale community over thirty years ago, and now there is a community health and wellness center, a doctor's office for the neighborhood, a legal center, an urban farm, affordable housing, a senior living center, and so much more.[36] All of this was located in a neighborhood that was historically one of the highest poverty areas in Chicago.

Our trip to Atlanta introduced us to the leadership team at Purpose Built Communities. Their framework included affordable housing, employment strategies, and a deep commitment to excellence in education. They also had significant backing of a high net worth business community to support their research-based initiatives.[37]

Our trip to the DC Dream Center—a ministry of National Community Church in Washington, DC—showed us that a church can engage in a community through intentional relationship building. By partnering with local nonprofit organizations, the Dream Center provides support and practical help for families living in a high-poverty community. Its efforts include an art center, dance studio, computer lab, basketball courts, recording studios, and much more.[38]

I traveled to Detroit with my friend Dionte to attend the Christian Community Development Association annual conference.[39] We were exposed to over three thousand like-minded practitioners who were deeply engaged in community development work across the world. We spent three days listening, learning, and growing as we sat under the teaching of people like Wayne Gordon, John Perkins, Shane Claiborne, and many more.

Every stop along the way, we were not arriving as experts trying to network, but students trying to learn and grow. Our relational circles grew exponentially as we took a season of intentional listening and learning. Many of the relationships that were formed over those four months of travel are still active and important relationships in our lives today.

The kingdom of God advances through relationships. And God graciously opened doors for us to be introduced to amazing people around the country who were deeply engaged in meaningful and lasting work in high-poverty communities.

One of the most important things I learned in my doctoral program was from Dr. Jim Vigil, the doctor of ministry director at Southeastern University.[40] He said, "Always remember that you are never the first person in the room. I want each of you to imagine that you are attending a dinner party as you enter your fields of study. You are entering rooms in which conversations have already been going for quite a while. Do not barge in with your thoughts and interrupt the flow of conversation. Listen to what everyone else is saying, and when it is natural, add your voice to the conversation."

Dr. Vigil was giving us an important lesson at the beginning of our studies, and I apply it to my work engaging topics of racial and economic justice every day. There are so many people who have invested deeply in this work long before I arrived in the room. I am called to listen and to learn from others, then add my voice as I have something substantive to say.

The season of listening and research that preceded the formation of Freedom Communities was absolutely vital to create a healthy and firm foundation for the work we hope to accomplish in the years to come. I do not know what God has in store for the future of this new work, but I do know that a common theme will be simple: everyone participates. This includes the residents of West Charlotte, the business community, and nonprofit organizations.

Dara and I created an executive summary of each of our trips and brought them back to prayerfully discuss with the business leaders who were investing into this season of research and relationship building. The more we explored best practices from around the country, the more the vision of Freedom Communities was forming in our hearts and minds. Each of us were deeply impacted by the choice to take our time to listen and learn from others who had gone before us in Chicago, Atlanta, Washington, DC, and Detroit.

I had no idea, however, that I would find one of the most significant puzzle pieces for the future work of Freedom Communities on Parramore Street in my childhood home-town—Orlando, Florida.

10

The City Beautiful

What does it look like for me to use what is in my hands
to create a movement that just might transform my city?
—Dr. Nicole Martin[41]

Dara and I arrived at the Lift Orlando office in downtown Orlando, and I immediately felt a sense of familiarity. I had walked around Lake Eola countless times in my life as a teenager growing up in the suburbs of Orlando. I had never noticed the mid-century, three story home that was now their headquarters overlooking the lake.

"I've been looking forward to this meeting," Eddy said. "The pastor from North Carolina who is studying generational poverty and wants to understand community development. Now that's interesting."

Eddy is the executive director at the center. [42] We hit it off right away.

"Our goal," Eddy said, "is to work hand in hand with longtime residents in downtown Orlando to redevelop their community. We do this by bringing together key stakeholders in the neighborhood. This includes residents, nonprofit organizations, and business leaders."

Eddy spent two hours with us that morning. We moved from comfortable brown leather couches in a sunroom overlooking the lake to the board room once the conversation really ramped up. "I didn't know we'd get this deep," he said. "We need a white board."

✱✱✱

This wasn't the first time I had been in the neighborhood where Lift Orlando focused their community development initiatives. The area was known to all of the locals as Parramore. That was the name of the main road that separated the Orlando Magic's arena from the high-poverty community across the street.

I grew up coming to Parramore every Saturday. My church had purchased an old U-Haul box truck to use for Sidewalk Sunday School. You read that right. Sidewalk Sunday School.

On a Saturday.

The idea was to bring what we experienced at church on Sundays in the northern suburbs of Orlando into the Parramore community on Saturday mornings. Looking back, this wasn't a great idea. At the time, however, this was the highlight of my week.

We painted the U-Haul truck bright yellow to make sure everyone could see us riding in from the suburbs each week. On the side of the truck, we painted puzzle pieces that had the cross in the center as "the main piece of the puzzle" to make sure everyone knew that our yellow cavalry of teenage students were centered around Jesus.

About twenty students and leaders would meet at the church each Saturday and load the truck with a simple sound system and supplies for games that we intended to play with kids in the Parramore neighborhood. We circled up and prayed that God would use our efforts for His glory and that miracles would happen because of our obedience.

After meeting at the church, we broke up into a handful of cars to make the twenty-minute drive from the northern suburbs to Parramore. Upon arrival, my friends and I would canvas the neighborhood with flyers inviting anyone who would listen to come join us at Sidewalk Sunday School. The adult leaders kept a few students back to set up a basic metal stage and a few microphones.

"Just look for the yellow puzzle truck."

That was certainly all of the instruction anyone needed as we passed out flyers.

After about thirty minutes of setting up and inviting as many people as possible, the show was ready to begin. We had a variety of evangelistic tools in the bag for Sidewalk Sunday School, but the human video was the main attraction. If you're not familiar with human videos, take a moment and just say a prayer of thanks to God.

The basic premise was that we would pick a powerful contemporary Christian song and choreograph our interpretation of the song. My assigned song was Steven Curtis Chapman's hit, *Saddle Up Your Horses*. I was ecstatic when I got the lead role.

This meant I got to lip-sync the most words.

If you're not familiar with Steven Curtis Chapman, you're probably in the same boat as every single resident of Parramore. Just imagine a mashup of country western pop and mid-90s acoustic power ballads.

The pinnacle of the human video involved a complex teenage pyramid built on the grass between the bright yellow puzzle truck and the brick government-funded housing complex on Parramore. I would climb to the top of the pyramid and then dramatically fall off into the arms of a few of my friends, only to burst back to the top of the pyramid.

If you can't interpret the meaning of this creative masterpiece, you can probably join the collection of thirty neighborhood residents who looked at me curiously as I smiled victoriously atop the pyramid of my peers shaking precariously beneath me.

Jesus came (in the puzzle truck), died (fell off the pyramid), and rose again (back on top of the pyramid). This was followed by a call to salvation by one of our adult leaders. This is the form of evangelism I experienced growing up.

And I loved it.

I think back now on this wild and weird practice and I am grateful because I formed some amazing albeit hilarious memories with my church friends during Sidewalk Sunday School. To this day, I still keep in contact with a few of them. But the truth is I looked forward to Sidewalk Sunday School because of the memories I was forming with my youth group friends each Saturday. Sidewalk Sunday School was way more about me and my friends than about the neighborhood residents. I am sad to say I do not remember the name of a single person in the Parramore community who we ministered to during my time as a sidewalk evangelist.

As Eddy got out the whiteboard markers to lay out Lift Orlando's strategy for effective community development, I realized more than ever that our human video stunt did next to nothing to help the Parramore community.

***

Eddy seemed to have endless energy that was fueled by a deep understanding of community-based redevelopment that placed the residents at the center of his work. Dara and I were fascinated as he filled an entire white board with various strategies that Lift Orlando was using to build relationships with neighbors. He talked about listening to their hopes, fears, and dreams. He introduced me to new principles in community development. We had a blast comparing notes and learning from each other.

Lift Orlando began when a group of community-minded business leaders gathered to explore a simple question: *Can the business community help solve some of our city's most complex social problems?* Their hope was that by leveraging their influence and aligning their corporate social responsibility efforts they could bring about lasting community transformation for Orlando's most vulnerable citizens. Dara and I were completely fascinated by the holistic way in which they supported families who were trying to break generational patterns of poverty.

Lift uses a model of community engagement called *collective impact* in which cross-sector organizations work toward a common agenda.[43] They also incorporate a philosophy of engagement called *place-based initiatives*.[44] These two philosophies would become foundational strategies for our work at Freedom Communities. Collective impact is accomplished when residents, business-owners, and nonprofit organizations come together for a common purpose. Place-based initiatives are accomplished by focusing effort and investment in one particular community over a long period of time.

Eddy said, "You have to acknowledge that you can't fix poverty everywhere, but you can make a difference if you focus your time, energy, and resources on a smaller geographic area. Concentrated areas of poverty require concentrated investment."

Focused effort on a concentrated area of poverty is key to the model at Lift Orlando. They operate within a three-quarter-mile radius that includes residential and commercial properties, abandoned lots, and foreclosed properties.

He continued, "When residents, business leaders, and nonprofits bring their resources together to one area, it leads to an impact much more dramatic than if those same resources were spread throughout the region."

Freedom Communities would eventually follow this model by choosing to focus on three neighborhoods in West Charlotte: Camp Greene, Enderly Park, and Ashley Park. The earliest days of our fledgling organization included significant amounts of time getting to know longtime residents. I reached out to the president of the Historic Camp Greene Neighborhood Association and offered to host their monthly community meeting at our church. I sat in the back of the room running the PowerPoint presentations for the meeting and learning from my new friends as they discussed the future of their neighborhood. My head was full of ideas for what I thought would benefit Camp Greene. However, I quickly learned that the best ideas came from the residents who called the neighborhood their home.

***

Eddy explained to me that Lift Orlando identified four areas in which they work directly with members of the community: housing, healthcare, education, and employment. Providing all four of these services helps families in low-income communities break the cycle of generational poverty and provide resources for them to live out their giftings and dreams.

"Business leaders should not be relegated to simply writing checks," he said. However, he also acknowledged that a group of businesspeople coming into an unfamiliar community with visions of redevelopment would need the genuine participation and partnership of the current residents. "We are doing everything we can to keep the residents in mind first and foremost," he said. "There has been an enormous amount of trust-building that has had to take place in the community. But we are starting to see some real measurable traction now."

Lift uses a framework called *asset-based community development*.[45] The basic premise of this approach acknowledges that each community boasts a unique combination of gifts, skills, and capacities of the community members with which to build its future.[46] Lift's team spent a considerable amount of time building an *asset map* that included existing elements of the community that the residents loved and wanted to remain as redevelopment began in their neighborhood.

Freedom Communities would follow the best practices of Lift by hiring a highly qualified real estate professional to create an asset map of every business, nonprofit organization, educational center, and location of influence within a one-mile radius of Camp Greene. To this day, the asset map continues to grow as new businesses move into the neighborhood and new developments are created.

One of our favorite parts of our trip to Orlando was connecting with the team at the Polis Institute. Phil Hissom founded this organization in response to the fact that cities were rapidly growing around the world. *Polis* is the Greek word for city, and the Polis Institute exists to ensure that the poor and disenfranchised are actively involved in shaping the stories of the cities in which they live.[47]

Dara and I were completely fascinated by the strategies Polis incorporated to ensure that Lift Orlando had a good understanding of the desires of the residents in the neighborhood in which they were working. Polis conducted over 1,500 door-to-door interviews and dozens of community gatherings to assess this grouping.[48] They collected data by hiring twelve residents of the community and trained them to professionally document their research.

Residents saw Lift Orlando employing their neighbors to conduct this work, and they gained a significant amount of momentum through their door-to-door effort. Trust began to form between residents and the leaders of the Lift Orlando organization because they chose to go the longer route of relationship building instead of just showing up and redeveloping the neighborhood. The team at the Polis Institute was able to identify the will of residents through a series of listening exercises. They engaged neighborhood leaders to co-create a plan to transform their community.

Eddy was beaming with excitement when he shared three questions that each resident was asked during the door-to-door interviews. He wrote them on the dry erase board as Dara and I feverishly tried to keep up in our note-taking and question asking.

- What do you love about your neighborhood?
- What do you want to stay the same in your neighborhood?
- What do you want to see changed in your neighborhood?

They compiled a list of existing assets in the community that were important to the long-time residents such as parks, three beautiful lakes, and favorite restaurants and shops. They also learned about properties that residents wanted to see redeveloped because of their reputation for violent crime and drug activity.

I was completely captivated when Eddy talked about taking this neighborhood-based research back to the group of businesspeople to get their perspective. One of the first initiatives that took place was the purchase and demolition of properties that had fallen into disrepair. One property in particular was purchased and torn down at the request of the neighbors. It was a dilapidated apartment complex known for drugs and prostitution. Lift redeveloped this property into a mixed-income housing development.

The unique combination of input and skills of everyone involved—residents, nonprofit leaders, and the business community—worked together to make a meaningful and sustainable investment in the neighborhood. Each group was needed for understanding the highest and best use of the available resources. I would later choose to base my entire doctoral dissertation around the same framework.[49]

Freedom Communities is a fairly new organization. We do not know what God will do in the years to come. After all, community development work is measured in generations. However, I do know that the early years of Freedom Communities has been impacted deeply by our trip to Orlando and the holistic community development framework that we learned from Lift Orlando and the Polis Institute. I am so grateful for their influence and friendship.

Following Lift's lead, one of the first major initiatives by Freedom Communities was to work with members of the community to create a coalition of organizations that represented the heartbeat of the West Charlotte neighborhoods. My eyes filled with tears as I stood in the back of the room and watched over eighty people packed into a community center co-create a vision for their neighborhood for the coming year.

Pastor Ken—the same pastor who welcomed me into the prayer group several years prior—stood to his feet at the end of the meeting and said, "I've been in this community for twenty years and I've never seen anything like this. This is an answer to prayer. We just spent all night discussing how we will work together to strengthen our community. My heart is full of joy."

***

I think we probably did more good than I can recall with our efforts with Sidewalk Sunday School. However, I am not rushing to purchase an old U-Haul to drive into the West Charlotte community any time soon.

Our best intentions are the most impactful when they are formed by the actual needs and desires of our community. Looking back, I am not sure if we ever asked if anyone wanted to observe me lip-syncing Steven Curtis Chapman songs at 9:00 o'clock on a Saturday morning on Parramore Street.

You don't need to do a doctoral program to engage in a season of listening and learning. You don't even need to become an expert on racial and economic injustice in our country. However, it would be deeply impacting if you cultivated a spirit of curiosity that left you with more questions than answers.

Jesus told us that the most important thing that we can do is to love God and neighbors with full passion. Imagine what would happen if everyone participated in listening, learning, and growing in our knowledge of why our communities are full of inequality and imbalances.

- How can you learn more about the neighborhoods in your community that are unlike yours?
- How can you engage in a season of listening, learning, and growing regarding systemic inequality in our country?
- How can your church participate in a *collective impact strategy* with other churches in your community?
- How can you learn about the history of neighborhoods in your city?

***

After being so impacted by observing his work in Orlando, I invited Phil Hissom to visit Charlotte and teach people in our neighborhood about holistic community development. He hosted a weekend seminar called *Dignity Serves* that teaches people how to serve and be served in every aspect of life.[50]

Phil said, "You have to think long-term when you are talking about community development. Each part is related to the other. You can't just address education if a child does not have stable housing. You have to think holistically, and that takes time."

Business leaders are familiar with thinking about return on their investments. I can't think of a single successful investor that I know who has seen sustained success by expecting quick returns from significant investments.

I often encourage businesspeople to view their investment into high-poverty communities the same way they view their financial investments. Let it marinate. Give the leaders you are investing into time to do it right. If you are going to invest a large amount of money into an effort that could make meaningful and measurable change in a community, let the experts do their part by creating the timeline and best practices for the organization.

We all need one another. And we all have a part to play.

***

Orlando is often referred to as *The City Beautiful*. Year-round summer temperatures, palm trees, and countless lakes create an incredible setting for residents and tourists alike. I always loved that term because it reminds me of the promise of God's perfect city in the book of Revelation when Jesus returns to establish His kingdom on earth as it is in heaven (Revelation 21).

The city of God is going to be so beautiful. But until we see that new heavenly city, I want to work toward a beautiful expression of life in my city.

Walter Brueggemann wrote a book called *Prophetic Imagination* that had an indelible impact on my life. I was challenged to see our culture for what it can be when it is centered around the prophetic example of Jesus. Brueggemann said, "The task of prophetic ministry is to nurture, nourish, and evoke a consciousness and perception alternative to the consciousness and perception of the dominant culture around us."[51] When you open yourself to receive God's vision for your community, He will give you some pieces to place in the puzzle that many others have been working on for years. You may have the piece that unlocks ten more for someone else.

***

Imagine a community in which all residents are unified in their vision for a beautiful expression of life.

Imagine a community in which people hold loosely to their possessions and generously share when their neighbors are in need.

Imagine unlocking the brilliance of children in all neighborhoods.

Imagine a community filled with people listening and learning to the stories and experiences of their neighbors.

Imagine a city where people from all different backgrounds gather together to fellowship, to enjoy a meal together, to worship together.

Imagine the city beautiful.

When I allow my imagination to run wild, I can imagine a beautiful city. (Lucky for you, there are no bright yellow U-Hauls full of suburban teens in this city.) Mark Batterson, in his book *Double Blessing,* said that seeking peace and prosperity of the city is accomplished by posturing ourselves with open hands and hearts.[52] As we open our hands to God, we simultaneously let go of that which we've held on to for too long. As we open our hearts to God, we can see His beauty across dividing lines.

It can be easy to view entire systemic change as overwhelming and impossible. However, the call to neighborliness is a personal call (loving God) that leads to genuinely beautiful communities (loving neighbors). Systemic change starts in the hearts of individuals. Your personal choice matters.

Cities can change because cities are made of people.

Systemic change takes a long time. Admittedly, I was hesitant to even write about the efforts we are undertaking with Freedom Communities because the organization is only a few years old. We are not experts. We are listening, learning, and growing every day. As I have observed and participated in the beginning stages of Freedom Communities, I would say that we are learning to work as the body of Christ.

We have an executive director that is a visionary leader and storyteller. She paints word pictures for us to see what we can accomplish when we work together. We have a staff that is uniquely gifted in areas of education, real estate, and direct work with families in the community. We have a diverse board of directors who are gifted in development, banking, academia, and communication. The bottom line is that no one can do this on their own.

I pray that the early days of Freedom Communities can be an encouragement to you, as well. We are doing our best to honor and learn from others who have gone before us. We are listening to the Holy Spirit as we try to envision the unique expression of neighborliness in our city. My prayer is that you will be able to pick up on some basic principles and then begin your own journey of listening, learning, and growing.

In time, I pray that you would have the courage to act on what you are learning.

God has given each one of us a handful of pieces for the puzzle. We need each other to put together the picture on the box cover. A picture of the City Beautiful.

11

Rebuild and Restore

We must learn to see a world Jesus has begun to flip right-side up so that those most despised as last and least valued are now first and most esteemed.
—Dr. Drew Hart, *Trouble I've Seen*

The book of Leviticus probably isn't the go-to for your daily devotions. I get that.

If you can stomach two full chapters about skin diseases (13–14) and another about bodily discharges (15), you can find some real beauty. The whole book is a detailed instruction manual on how to live in the context of a worshiping community. A few of the gems include:

- "Do not twist justice in legal matters by favoring the poor or being partial to the rich and powerful. Always judge people fairly" (19:15).
- "Do not seek revenge or bear a grudge against anyone among your people, but love your neighbor as yourself" (19:18, NIV).

- "When a foreigner resides among you in your land, do not mistreat them. The foreigner residing among you must be treated as your native-born. Love them as yourself, for you were foreigners in Egypt" (19:33–34, NIV).

I love the book of Leviticus because it shows how much God cares about the way we treat one another. We are encouraged to treat the rich and the poor equally. Foreigners are supposed to be shown hospitality and kindness. Forgiveness should flow to others in the same way you would hope someone would forgive you. We even get instructions on how to care for one another if someone has a contagious skin disease.

If that's not a perfect picture of neighborliness, I don't know what is.

In fact, all the books of the law support neighborliness. In Exodus, expressing love to neighbors also includes showing kindness to enemies. Exodus 23:4–5 says, "If you come across your enemy's ox or donkey wandering off, be sure to return it. If you see the donkey of someone who hates you fallen down under its load, do not leave it there; be sure to help them with it" (NIV).

The clear expectation from God is that loving a neighbor is not dependent on proximity or nationality. Loving neighbors means loving each person created in the image of God . . . and helping them with their injured donkey or whatever the modern-day equivalent is.

Misguided Affection

The sheer volume of historical context for the topic of neighborliness is unmistakably woven throughout the Old Testament. In the book of Isaiah, the prophet speaks of neighborliness in his rebuke of the nation of Israel after the people misdirected their affection. Seven hundred years before the earthly life and ministry of Jesus, the prophet Isaiah was called by God to rebuke communities of worshipers who were not exhibiting a spirit of neighborliness and were distracted and unfocused in their worship toward God. Isaiah 58:1–14 describes a group of business leaders who had taken time away from their normal work day abstaining from food and singing songs of praise and commitment to God. Sounds like a good thing, right?

Not so fast.

These business leaders took time off work to worship God, only to find out that God was terribly unpleased with their religious activity. Their excitement to express very public and animated acts of worship was detestable to the Lord because of their lack of care for the overlooked and marginalized in their community. Isaiah 1:16–17 says, "Take your evil deeds out of my sight; stop doing wrong. Learn to do right; seek justice. Defend the oppressed. Take up the cause of the fatherless; plead the case of the widow" (NIV).

The prophet was irate. Isaiah emphatically rebukes the worshipers in this passage because they valued the practices of corporate fasting and worship more than they valued genuine and equitable relationships with their employees. He challenges this group to fast from their inequitable behaviors that brought division to God's people and marginalized the most vulnerable members of the community. God is using Isaiah to call the worshiping community into a deeper understanding of His heart for an inclusive and neighborly community that makes room for all who long to worship alongside one another.

Isaiah continues as God's mouthpiece, "Yet they act so pious. They come to the Temple every day and seem delighted to learn all about me. They act like a righteous nation that would never abandon the laws of its God. They ask me to take action on their behalf, pretending they want to be near me" (Isaiah 58:2).

Pretending they want to be near me.

Isaiah called out the community of believers for neglecting their marginalized neighbors at the same time that they were making very bold and very public declarations of their commitment to God. Christian theologian Walter Brueggemann said, "These two verses establish the core problem of the community, namely, a hypocritical gap between the actual conduct of the community and the intention of the community expressed in worship."[53]

Can you see how easy it can be to be misguided in our affection? The language in this passage is direct and offers biting criticism toward people who genuinely believed they were worshiping God with a right heart and spirit. However, God was not simply focused on their expression of love for Him. God desired their expression of love to also include love for their neighbors.

Can you see how clearly that connects to the greatest commandment in Mark 12:28–34? God's heart was not moved by all the religious fervor and activity in this worship gathering. He chose instead to focus His attention on the fact that during their worship experience, they were still involved in the exploitation and unfair treatment of their community.[54]

The people responded in Isaiah 58:3, "We have fasted before you!" they say. "Why aren't you impressed? We have been very hard on ourselves, and you don't even notice it!" Isaiah responds, "It's because you are fasting to please yourselves, Even while you fast, you keep oppressing your workers."

The back and forth here between the people and God shows that God was not interested in their self-serving displays of affection. He longed for their hearts to match His heart. Extravagant worship gatherings would never replace His desire for peace and justice for neighbors in their community who have been oppressed. Their worship was self-serving because it excluded the overlooked and marginalized. Their worship was half-hearted because they wanted to hold onto their power, wealth, and possessions, which reminds me of another story in the Bible.

You Are What You Love

Jesus could see this man's wealth from a mile away—his gold jewelry glimmered in the noonday sun. He looked young, younger than Jesus at least. When the rich young man approached Jesus and His disciples, he greeted them with respect. Then he immediately got down to business: "What should I do to inherit eternal life?" (Luke 18:18).

Jesus could tell that the man who stood before Him was committed to his faith and eager to learn. He was a man who was used to getting what he wanted, but it seemed by his inquiry he was looking for one thing that no amount of money could buy. Jesus responded by sharing some of the basic and most prominent commands given to the religious community during this time.

- Do not murder.
- Do not commit adultery.
- Do not steal.
- Do not testify falsely.
- Do not cheat anyone.
- Honor your father and mother.
- Love your neighbor as yourself.

"I've obeyed all these commandments since I was young," the rich young man replied (Luke18:21). Instinctively, the man knew that the religious rules of the day were left lacking. He had feasted on the rules of religion, yet he was still hungry. He needed to know more.

Jesus replied, "Go, sell all your possessions and give to the poor, and you will have treasure in heaven. Then come, follow me." When the man heard this, "he went away sad, because he had great wealth" (Matthew 19:21–22 NIV). The affections of his heart were exposed by the command of Jesus to give up everything to follow Him.

Jesus knew that when the wealthy young man chased Him down to ask about salvation, the young man would first have to deal with his love of money. As James K.A. Smith says in his book *You Are What You Love,* "Jesus is a teacher who doesn't just want to inform our intellect but forms our very loves. He isn't content to simply deposit new ideas into your mind; he is after nothing less than your wants, your loves, your longings."[55] The story shows us that the young man had already followed a majority of the religious rules of the day. However, in order for him to truly know and love and follow Jesus, the rich young man would have to conquer his love of money. Jesus knew that the man could not serve two masters with the same devotion.[56] The rich man was disheartened by the choice he had to make between caring for his wealth and caring for the things of God. Just like the business leaders in the book of Isaiah, the young man was willing to worship God in a myriad of other ways, just not with his position, possessions, or money.

I believe, whether it is stated or not, God is always leading us to take an inventory of our desires. Ronald Sider said, "Either Jesus and his kingdom matter so much that we are ready to sacrifice everything else, including our possessions, or we are not serious about Jesus."[57]

Would you give up *everything* in order to follow Jesus?

The answer to that question uncovers your true affection.

The Spirit of Mammon

Matthew 6:24 says, "No one can serve two masters. For you will hate one and love the other; you will be devoted to one and despise the other. You cannot serve God and be enslaved to money." The King James version actually personifies money by giving it a name: mammon.

French theologian Jacques Ellul wrote a book called *Money and Power* that explored the dynamic that is presented in Matthew 6:24. He said, "We absolutely must not minimize the parallel Jesus draws between God and mammon." He continues, "God as a person and mammon as a person find themselves in conflict. Mammon can be a master the same way God is; that is, mammon can be a personal master."

The spirit of mammon can be depicted by one very familiar word to all of us: greed. The love of money results in the insatiable desire for more. The deception of the ladder of success is that there is no end to "climbing the ladder." The love of money breeds a feeling of scarcity. Ellul said, "Mammon shows himself to be a lying power by constantly deceiving us. He arouses desires which he never satisfies."[58]

The opposing characters of God and money share the same characteristic: they need to be your everything. God is jealous, which means He wants no other gods to come before Him; He wants to be, and deserves to be, the sole recipient of your adoration and honor. When He is first in your heart, His love overflows into every aspect of your life and you naturally serve and love others. Mammon is also a jealous god. When he is first in your life, money, greed, and self-sufficiency take precedence and become the motivation for every thought and action. Love for money naturally leads us into isolation because it impacts our relationships by viewing others as commodities to help us achieve our next goal. The spirit of mammon is in direct opposition of the spirit of God, and the spirit of mammon is in direct opposition of the spirit of neighborliness.

Money can never bring the happiness our culture promises. Only a life that is found whole and complete in Jesus can satisfy the longing of the human heart. By introducing God and money as opposing characters, Jesus is using language that digs deep past the surface and into our affections. He draws a clear line in the sand. This is not casual indifference. Jesus is clearly stating that a person will hate one master and love the other. God or money. Who has your love?

**

If we look closely at our desires and motivations, I think we will see that we aren't too far from the business leaders in Isaiah or the rich young ruler in the book of Matthew. The spirit of mammon has been keeping us from loving God and our neighbors fully for centuries.

I recognize the spirit of mammon in my ministry. I have felt the temptation to insatiably chase after levels of numeric and financial growth in my church. The lie from the Enemy is that satisfaction can be found by reaching certain numeric and financial benchmarks. However, I have found that peace and tranquility can only be found at the feet of Jesus. Growth is not bad or ungodly, but growth as a god is sinful.

Instead of finding security in their status as a son or daughter of the King, many leaders are caught in the unattainable pursuit of success defined by accumulation of accomplishments and wealth. Greed often tries to ensnare us with the false promise of peace and security. We are tempted to push the boundaries of health and rest in order to achieve the next level of perceived success. The next level leads to the next, and there is never an end because the spirit of mammon has infiltrated our definition of success.

Flourishing Communities

In order to cross dividing lines and love our neighbors well, we must ask the question: In what ways are we pursuing extravagant self-serving worship experiences while ignoring the cries of our neighbors who are desperate for justice?

In his book *Rich Christians in an Age of Hunger,* Ronald Sider challenged church leaders and churchgoers to evaluate themselves regarding their care for those who are poor and marginalized. He said, "Is there the same balance and emphasis on justice for the poor and oppressed in our programs as there is in Scripture?"[59]

Sadly, all too often the answer to that question is a resounding no.

If Isaiah were to visit your church or small group today, what would his message be?

The worshiping community in Isaiah 58 thought that they were on track in their devotion to God, only to come to the startling realization that their relationship with Him was not integrated or unified. I truly believe the worshipers weren't intentionally being disingenuous in their worship, which is why we need to allow God to search us, know us, and see if there is any offensive way in us. Even though the people genuinely believed that these acts of worship should win them special favor with God, their true motivation was to gain ground in the struggle for power, position, and pos-

sessions.[60] God communicated through Isaiah, in no uncertain terms, that He saw past their religious activity and
into their sin-filled hearts. Through Isaiah, He lovingly and
forcefully called them to repentance. Just as Jesus did with
the rich young ruler 700 years later. And just as Jesus is calling us to do in this present moment.

Isaiah 58:6–7 describes the acts of worship that God is
interested in: "Free those who are wrongly imprisoned; light-
en the burden of those who work for you. Let the oppressed
go free, and remove the chains that bind people. Share your
food with the hungry, and give shelter to the homeless. Give
clothes to those who need them, and do not hide from rela-
tives who need your help."

The prophet asked the community of employers to treat
their employees in a way that valued them as human be-
ings, not just as commodities that could bring profitability
to their organization. He asked those who have gained positions of power to allow those that have been oppressed to
go free. He was requiring that the worshiping community
behave in a way that justice for everyone would be a reality;
a community free of greed, so there would be room for love.
God is asking those same questions to anyone who holds
any sort of position of influence or power today.

- Do you treat your employees or subordinates
  with kindness and respect?
- Do you actively use your position to ensure they
  are treated with fairness?
- Are you paying your employees appropriately?

- Have you actively taken an interest in their lives beyond what they do for you?

Verse 8–9 reads, "Then your salvation will come like the dawn, and your wounds will quickly heal. Your godliness will lead you forward, and the glory of the LORD will protect you from behind. Then when you call, the LORD will answer; 'Yes, I am here,' he will quickly reply. Remove the heavy yoke of oppression."

I love the way God so obviously ignores their pious acts of worship, yet when they turn their attention to an expression of faith that includes loving God and neighbors, it says *He will quickly reply.* This shows that God's heart is moved when we are properly expressing both halves of the greatest commandment.

Verses 10–11 become more prescriptive and direct in the expectation that God has for the worshiping community to care for others. Isaiah said, "Feed the hungry and help those in trouble. Then your life will shine out from the darkness, and the darkness around you will be as bright as noon. The LORD will guide you continually, giving you water when you are dry and restoring your strength. You will be like a well-watered garden, like an ever-flowing spring."

The imagery here is absolutely stunning. This is only one example of many in Scripture that describes naturally flourishing vegetation. I believe God uses this type of imagery to show that when we align our religious fervor with His perfect plan, our communities begin to naturally flourish with relationships and dividing lines disappear. If we truly love God with full passion, the natural outflow will be love for and equitable relationships with others.

Isaiah continues by talking about the community-wide reform that is needed in order to experience flourishing communities: "Some of you will rebuild the deserted ruins of your cities. Then you will be known as a rebuilder of walls and a restorer of homes" (v. 58:12).

I am fascinated by that phrase *some of you*. It seems as if Isaiah is stating that in a worshiping community, there are some who will have the capacity and the imagination to be able to envision the ability to restore and rebuild entire cities.

- *Some of you* will be anointed to assess the systems and frameworks of entire communities and discern an equitable path forward for your city.
- *Some of you* will be called to inhabit places of influence and power in government to shape practices that cultivate a spirit of neighborliness in your city.

This passage doesn't mean that any position is more or less important than another. However, it does seem to state that there are some who are going to be uniquely anointed to bring about systemic change through positions of leadership and influence. Is this you? Does your heart beat a little faster when you read Isaiah 58:12?

This was the passage God spoke over my life the night I felt the call to bring an organization to life in West Charlotte that would holistically care for families that were trapped in the devastating pattern of generational poverty. I read the passage and my heart was gripped. My heart is still gripped.

That moment led to a series of prayers in which I asked God to give me a plan for how we could impact the neighborhood surrounding Center City Church. The result of those prayers was the basic framework for the work that we now do with Freedom Communities. We provide access to education, employment, healthcare, and affordable housing for families in West Charlotte.

Community-wide reform starts with asking God to search your heart and reveal anything that does not satisfy Him. If you allow Jesus to change your heart, He can give you the plan that will impact others and lead to flourishing communities.

***

The final few verses of this passage always bothered me. Not because of the content as much as the placement. Isaiah 58:1–12 is a stunning rebuke of a community that is followed by genuine repentance. There is a breathtaking picture painted of a naturally flourishing community that includes people being set apart by God to bring about amazing, citywide reform. And then in verses 13 and 14, Isaiah talks about rest.

That can't be right, can it? A lesson on the Sabbath after this profound passage on rebuke, repentance, neighborliness, and restoring an entire city?

I was telling my friend, Steve, about my annoyance with Isaiah's encouragement to rest right after this powerful passage, and Steve said, "David, it makes total sense. Every time that God leads us into the rhythm of work, He always follows that with a regular rhythm of rest."

Verses 13–14 say, "Keep the Sabbath day holy. Don't pursue your own interests on that day, but enjoy the Sabbath and speak of it with delight as the LORD's holy day. Honor the Sabbath in everything you do on that day, and don't follow your own desires or talk idly. Then the LORD will be your delight. I will give you great honor and satisfy you with the inheritance I promised to your ancestor Jacob. I, the LORD, have spoken!"

Don't pursue your own interests on that day. God calls us to rest in order to surrender the desires we naturally veer toward when we aren't taking time to reflect. It is important to rest so we can see if mammon is present in any of our desires, even our desires to restore and rebuild community. After such a thrilling journey from repentance to joy, God lovingly reminds us that we should not attempt to do all of this reparation work without choosing the discipline of setting aside time to rest, reflect, and allow the Spirit to reenergize our work.

We rest because we can never accomplish it all on our own.

We rest because we choose to actively resist the unending pace of the world to require more and more of our time.

We rest because the spirit of self-sufficiency and our insatiable need for more is defeated by our direct reliance on God, not our ability to push through and overcome on our own.

We rest to delight in God.

12

Already and Not Yet

The act of bringing the world into existence is a
continual process. God called the world into being,
and that call goes on.
—**Abraham Joshua Heschel**, *The Sabbath, Its Meaning for
the Modern Man*

"Dara, I can't breathe. Please pray for me."

I was doubled over on the floor of our family friends'
fourteenth-story condo in Daytona Beach, Florida. They had
generously given me a few days at their beautiful oceanfront
condo for a writing retreat. I was supposed to be spending
my time organizing the outline for my doctoral dissertation
and beginning to write the first draft of chapter one.

However, I couldn't even stand up.

Moments earlier, I was staring at a floor-to-ceiling outline of the dissertation I was supposed to write on the topic
of race, economics, and friendship. I had filled over twenty
pages of huge Post-it notes and hung them on the wall. The
empty Microsoft Word page was taunting me as I prepared

to write. And that's when I started to feel my stomach turn. "You are not the person to write this," the familiar voice inside my head said to me. "There has to be someone better to write this."

The assault continued.

I stood up, stared at the wall, and started to pray. I was overwhelmed because, for the first time, my research was laid out in front of me. Three years of research highlighting inequitable treatment of my neighbors. The same system that was set up for my success was pushing aside and marginalizing my friends. I couldn't stop staring at the wall. The familiar voice of insecurity continued to ravage my spirit.

"This is too big," I said out loud. "I am the absolute last person who needs to be talking about this stuff. I still have so much to learn and I have made so many mistakes. I am no expert on bringing people together across racial and economic lines. I can't do this."

I placed my hands on my knees and I started to audibly cry. "God, please." I was at a loss for words. "Please let someone else say this. There are so many smart people who are more eloquent and understand the issues better. Please, God, I am not the right one for this."

I dropped into the fetal position on the tile floor.

"Dara, I can't breathe. Please pray."

I sent that text to Dara and then realized she probably thought I was dying.

"I am doubled over on the ground crying and I'm totally out of breath. It hurts, love."

"God called you to this," she replied. "He will give you the words."

She always says the best things. I could sense the resolve in her text.

I don't know what happened, but all of a sudden, the pain in my stomach went away. I felt peace fill my heart, mind, and spirit in a way that I have only felt a few times in my life. The Holy Spirit whispered to me, "Start with your own heart. Start with your own heart and then share this message with one person at a time."

Systems can change because systems are made of people. That is the phrase my friend Peter used in his book about gentrification and inequality, *How to Kill a City*.[61] If individuals do not change, systems won't change. I moved from the fetal position on the tile to my knees.

"I will do it, God," I said. "But I need to know you are with me."

I stood to my feet.

"My words will never be enough to change anyone's heart," I prayed, "but you can, God."

I felt peace and confidence fill my heart, soul, mind, and spirit. My insecurity was crucified that day. Sure, insecurity tries to reemerge every single day, but I chose to remember how I rose from my breaking point into the fullness of God. My inadequate words point to the all-powerful message of Christ.

My call is to share the message of neighborliness one person at a time.

A PICTURE OF HOPE

Theologians refer to our time on the earth as the *already and not yet.*

We experience forgiveness, freedom, and healing when we fix our eyes on Jesus. However, we are easily distracted from His peace and promises when we scroll through social media or turn on the news. The hatred, violence, sickness, pain, and anger shouts in our faces.

Contrastingly, Revelation 21 paints a prophetic picture of hope. There will come a day with there is no more political divisiveness and systemic inequality. Family and friends will no longer be lost to sickness. Anger and rage will be replaced with unity and joy. Permanently.

Jesus taught us to pray that the kingdom of God would come to the earth *as it is in heaven.* The same peace and unity that is experienced in heaven is to be practiced here on earth. We experience the beautiful kingdom of God right now—*the already*—when we behave in the way that we will behave in heaven. When we see each other, work past our differences, and love each other well. We experience the brokenness of this world—*the not yet*—when we allow our differences to drive us apart. Divisiveness and disunity have no place in the beautiful kingdom of God. And they have no place as we practice the kingdom of God on earth right now as it is in heaven.

Worship fills the air like a beautiful fragrance as Jesus establishes His kingdom on this earth. Furthermore, every picture that I see in Revelation of a worshiping community includes *every nation and tongue.* There is a day coming that we will all worship together with one heart and one voice.

If there was one thing I would leave you with after our time together, it is the charge to explore your heart and courageously look inward before you try to engage in relationships across dividing lines. When you identify and reconcile things that have kept you from fulfilling both halves of the greatest commandment, you will find you are living a whole life.

Jesus gave us a clear pathway to finding friendship across dividing lines. Love God. Love your neighbors. This is the culmination of already and not yet.

We can practice the reality of *already* in the midst of the *not yet*.

***

The culmination of my doctoral program was a seminar that I hosted on the topic of neighborliness. We packed the main auditorium at Center City Church with people who were hungry to learn how they could explore the topics of race, economics, and friendship.

During the third session, my friend Corey led us in a time of worship. I looked to my right and I saw Gerald, a resident from Camp Greene. He was standing next to Timothy, a resident of Bryant Park. Tears filled my eyes as I realized that every measurable sociological statistic would say that Gerald and Timothy would not have much in common. However, they had been sitting together throughout the entire seminar learning about the same topics from two extremely different perspectives.

I was overwhelmed when I saw them, side by side, lifting their hands in worship to God. The *already* and *not yet*. These are the moments when we are able to get brief glimpses of the unity, joy, and perfection of heaven while we are still experiencing the reality of the brokenness of this earth.

The reason Gerald and Timothy could worship together is because they learned how to cross a two-lane road called Berryhill Avenue and enter into a flourishing community of friends at Center City Church. They built a friendship by intentionally engaging across lines that generally divide.

I thought of the picture of hope Revelation 21 holds, of what it will look like when the kingdom of God is established on earth as it is in heaven. There will be no more pain, crying, sickness, or division. As Gerald and Timothy raised their hands in worship, I realized I was experiencing a brief glimpse of heaven on earth. I watched in holy silence as The Tale of Two Cities became the unfolding story of the City Beautiful.

I was seeing the beauty of God across dividing lines.

Closing Prayer: The Gloria

Glory be to God the Father,

God the Son, and God the Holy Spirit.

As it was in the beginning, so it is now,

and so it ever shall be, world without end.

Alleluia. Amen.

Neighborliness Group Study

My prayer is that the end of this book would be the beginning of the conversation.

Our relationship with Jesus begins as an inward journey that naturally leads to exploring how our faith is expressed in the context of community. I encourage you to share the next part of this journey with a group of friends.

The following study guide includes suggestions on how to organize conversations. I have provided conversation prompts, but feel free to let your discussions flow freely and naturally. Depending on each person's upbringing, the way this book is processed will be very different. As you listen and learn, you'll see that each person can help the group explore the spirit of neighborliness from various perspectives.

The Bible describes the posture and character of folks who are learning to express the spirit of neighborliness. We should be quick to listen, slow to speak, and slow to get angry (James 1:19). Let curiosity lead the way as you hear the thoughts and experiences of your friends. Extend and receive grace freely. God is honored when His children pursue unity.

I am hopeful that this book will give you tools to have meaningful conversations that lead to new friendships as you find the beauty of God across dividing lines.

INTRODUCTION
The Day I Opened My Eyes

Keep on loving each other as brothers and sisters. Don't forget to show hospitality to strangers, for some who have done this have entertained angels without realizing it! Remember those in prison, as if you were there yourself. Remember also those being mistreated, as if you felt their pain in your own bodies.
Hebrews 13:1–3

Discussion Prompts:

1. Why did you decide to read this book and participate in this conversation?
2. What stood out to you after reading the introduction?
3. Can you relate to the idea of silence?
4. How do you respond when you witness injustice?
5. Do you have a person or group of people you feel comfortable engaging with in challenging conversations?

Next Step: Start with prayer. Pray that God would help you to see the beauty of God across dividing lines.

CHAPTER ONE
The Other Half of the Greatest Commandment

And you must love the Lord your God with all your heart, all your soul, all your mind, and all your strength. The second is equally important: "Love your neighbor as yourself." No other commandment is greater than these.
Mark 12:30–31

Discussion Prompts:

1. What stood out to you after reading Chapter One?
2. Define *neighbor* in your own words.
3. Define *neighborliness* in your own words.
4. Do my friendships reflect the diversity in my city? Why or why not?
5. What are some practical ways to love your neighbor?

> Next Step: Continue to learn. Choose one of the recommended resources to read or watch in the next week.

CHAPTER TWO
A Tale of Two Cities

Do to others whatever you would like them to do to you. This is the essence of all that is taught in the law and the prophets.
Matthew 7:12

Discussion Prompts:

1. What stood out to you after reading Chapter Two?
2. We explored the stories of Andrea, Jasmine, Jamila, Eric, and Grandma Sadie. Which of these people do you relate to the most?
3. What comes to mind when you hear the word *gentrification*?
4. Describe *helping networks* in your own words.
5. How can your faith work for everyone around you?

Next Step: Listen to the song "Gentrify" by an artist named Propaganda to get an overview of gentrification. Look up the lyrics and follow along.

CHAPTER THREE
A Look Inward

Search me, O God, and know my heart; test me and know
my anxious thoughts. Point out anything in me that offends
you, and lead me along the path of everlasting life.
Psalm 139:23–24

Discussion Prompts:

1. What stood out to you after reading Chapter Three?
2. Describe *inattentional blindness* in your own words.
3. Describe *implicit bias* in your own words.
4. What is the difference between *not racist* and *antiracist*?
5. Discuss Dr. Brian Blount's idea that we must identify cultural boundaries in need of kingdom trespass.

> Next Step: Pray the same way David did in Psalm 139:23–24. After asking God to search your heart, write down the areas you sense the Holy Spirit is challenging you to address from this reading.

CHAPTER FOUR
Reconsidering Reconciliation and Inclusion

*After this I saw a vast crowd, too great to count, from every
nation and tribe and people and language, standing in front
of the throne and before the Lamb.*
Revelation 7:9

Discussion Prompts:

1. What stood out to you after reading Chapter Four?
2. Throughout history, how has the church been complicit in racism and inequality?
3. Throughout history, how has the church been courageous in addressing racism and inequality?
4. Discuss the difference between *racial reconciliation* and *racial conciliation*.
5. Do you believe that racial representation is the same as unity? Why or why not?

Next Step: Watch Mark Charles' TED Talk, "The Truth Behind 'We the People'–the Three Most Misunderstood Words in US History."[62]

CHAPTER FIVE
From One Generation to the Next

*Let each generation tell its children of your mighty acts; let
them proclaim your power.*
Psalm 145:4

Discussion Prompts:

1. What stood out to you after reading Chapter Five?
2. Desmond Tutu said that if you are neutral in situations of injustice, you have chosen the side of the oppressor. Explain why you agree or disagree.
3. The rich and the poor are neighbors in cities. Does proximity naturally lead to relationships?
4. What are ways you can creatively cultivate opportunities to learn about racial and economic inequality?
5. Would you be willing to sit with a friend at Woolworth's lunch counter?

Next Step: Watch Dr. Lucretia Berry's TED Talk,
"Children Will Light Up the World if We Don't Keep
Them in the Dark."[63]

CHAPTER SIX
Learning to Lament

I am sick at heart. How long, O LORD, until you restore me? Return, O LORD, and rescue me. Save me because of your unfailing love.
Psalm 6:3–4

Discussion Prompts:

1. What stood out to you after reading Chapter Six?
2. How many songs can you think of that express God-honoring lament?
3. Describe and discuss the meaning of healthy lament.
4. Jemar Tisby said that racism in America has *adapted* since the abolishment of slavery. Do you agree or disagree? Explain why or why not.
5. Have you ever corporately or personally grieved the loss of somebody you didn't know?

Next Step: Watch Ava DuVernay's documentary 13TH.

CHAPTER SEVEN
We Belong to One Another

God works in different ways, but it is the same God who does the work in all of us. A spiritual gift is given to each of us so we can help each other.
1 Corinthians 12:6–7

Discussion Prompts:

1. What stood out to you after reading Chapter Seven?
2. How can language like *those people* and *them* create unhealthy distance between neighbors?
3. How do events like natural disasters and global pandemics highlight underlying issues of inequality in our society?
4. How can you embody the love of Christ to your neighbors?
5. How would your city be different if everyone truly belonged to one another?

Next Step: Have a conversation with a friend outside of this study group about one thing you are learning.

CHAPTER EIGHT
Toxic Charity

There is joy for those who deal justly with others and always
do what is right.
Psalm 106:3

Discussion Prompts:

1. What stood out to you after reading Chapter Eight?
2. Describe *toxic charity* in your own words.
3. Discuss the different perspectives of Roman, Todd, David, Lisa, and Michael.
4. How can a posture of humility and curiosity lead to healthy expressions of volunteerism?
5. How can outreach programs become more meaningful if relationships are built between donors, volunteers, and the recipients of needed resources?

> Next Step: Make a list of three nonprofit organizations in your city that align with your interest and passion. Familiarize yourself with their work in the community. Pray about your potential involvement.

CHAPTER NINE
Everyone Participates

Now these are the gifts Christ gave to the church: the apostles,
the prophets, the evangelists, and the pastors and teachers.
Their responsibility is to equip God's people to do his work
and build up the church, the body of Christ.
Ephesians 4:11–12

Discussion Prompts:

1. What stood out to you after reading Chapter Nine?
2. Describe *social capital* in your own words.
3. Discuss how education can equal action.
4. Is God biased toward the rich or the poor? Discuss why or why not?
5. What is your first response when you come into close proximity with someone in need?

Next Step: Prayerfully narrow the list of three nonprofit organizations down to one that you can engage in relationship and service. Continue to pray that the Holy Spirit would lead you to discern when and how to best support their mission.

CHAPTER TEN
The City Beautiful

Pray like this: Our Father in heaven, may your name be kept holy. May your Kingdom come soon. May your will be done on earth, as it is in heaven.
Matthew 6:9–10

Discussion Prompts:

1. What stood out to you after reading Chapter Ten?
2. Describe and discuss *asset-based community development*, *collective impact*, and *place-based initiatives*.
3. How can your church participate in a *collective impact strategy* with other churches and organizations in your community?
4. If you created an asset map of your community, what would be included?
5. Describe your version of The City Beautiful.

Next Step: Slowly read and reflect on 2 Chronicles 7:14. Write a prayer and declare it over your city.

CHAPTER ELEVEN
Restore and Rebuild

No, this is the kind of fasting I want: Free those who are wrongly imprisoned; lighten the burden of those who work for you. Let the oppressed go free, and remove the chains that bind people.
Isaiah 58:6

Discussion Prompts:

1. What stood out to you after reading Chapter Eleven?
2. How was the corporate fast displeasing to God in Isaiah 58?
3. Why did the rich young ruler experience sadness?
4. How has the influence of the spirit of mammon led to decisions in your life? How does the Sabbath directly oppose the spirit of mammon?
5. Isaiah 58:12 describes a unique calling to those who are anointed to bring about citywide reform. If this resonates in your spirit, discuss this with your group.

Next Step: Practice Sabbath rest. For more information on the Sabbath, Abraham Joshua Heschel's book, The Sabbath, is a powerful story of a family that centered their week around the rhythm of work and rest.

CHAPTER TWELVE
Already and Not Yet

He will wipe away every tear from their eyes, and there will
be no more death or sorrow or crying or pain.
All these things are gone forever.
Revelation 21:4

Discussion Prompts:

1. What stood out to you after reading Chapter Twelve?
2. How do you see the *already* being expressed in your community?
3. How do you see the *not yet* being expressed in your community?
4. If neighborliness is expressed one person at a time, where can you begin?
5. Describe one of the most challenging and encouraging things you will take away from reading *Neighborliness: Finding the Beauty of God Across Dividing Lines.*

Next Step: Choose to engage. Refuse to ignore.

Neighborliness in Your Church

You can visit www.neighborliness.com to see how my friends at Radiant Printing and I have designed materials for further discussion. Resources include:

- A discussion guide for book clubs, churches, businesses, and organizations.
- A churchwide campaign that includes a four-week sermon series with sermon notes, full-sermon videos, and promotional graphics and videos.
- A citywide campaign for churches to explore *Neighborliness* with multiple congregations at the same time.

RECOMMENDED RESOURCES

Recommended Reading

I recommend any of the books mentioned in *Neighborliness*. However, some are easier than others to engage in if you are at or near the beginning of your journey. The books listed below are recommended to inspire readers that want to go from reading *Neighborliness* to a practical next step.

The Color of Compromise: The Truth About the American Church's Complicity in Racism
Jemar Tisby

How to Kill a City: Gentrification, Inequality, and the Fight for the Neighborhood
Peter Moskowitz

I'm Still Here: Black Dignity in a World Made for Whiteness
Austin Channing Brown

Just Mercy: A Story of Justice and Redemption
Bryan Stevenson

One Blood: Parting Words to the Church on Race
John Perkins

Rethinking Incarceration: Advocating for Justice that Restores
Dominique DuBois Gilliard

Rich Christians in an Age of Hunger: Moving from Affluence to Generosity
Ronald Sider

Trouble I've Seen: Changing the Way the Church Views Racism
Dr. Drew G.I. Hart

Unsettling Truths: The Ongoing, Dehumanizing Legacy of the Doctrine of Discovery
Mark Charles and Soong-Chan Rah

The Very Good Gospel: How Everything Wrong Can Be Made Right
Lisa Sharon Harper

When Helping Hurts: How to Alleviate Poverty without Hurting the Poor . . . and Yourself
Steve Corbett and Brian Fikkert

Recommended Listening

Codeswitch by NPR
Footnotes with Jemar Tisby
The Red Couch Podcast
Inverse Podcast by Dr. Drew Hart & Jarrod McKenna
Revisionist History by Malcolm Gladwell
    Season 1, Episodes 4–6

Recommended Seminar

Dignity Serves
The Polis Institute

Dignity Serves is a paradigm-shifting, deeply impactful experience that teaches how to both serve and be served with dignity in every aspect of life. Since 2008, it has helped thousands of people serve others more effectively, using interactive exercises and real-world examples to help participants apply key principles to their personal lives and to the programs they take part in.

The principles of the course are derived from Scripture and built on the foundation that every person is created in the image of God. Every person possesses dignity. The course is made available through host organizations and is taught by Polis-trained facilitators.

For more information, visit www.dignityserves.com.

Recommended Online Resources

What Lies Between Us: Fostering First Steps Toward Racial Healing
Dr. Lucretia Carter Berry

Dr. Berry has cultivated an online membership platform that provides education, encouragement, and community.

Through three simple stages, participants in the Brownicity community are guided through a process from fundamental understanding to practicing transformative change in their spheres of influence.

Additionally, Brownicity offers a small group study called *What Lies Between Us,* an in-depth study that takes participants through an enlightening and introspective journey towards recovering from the lies of race to progress towards racial healing. Online training for parents is available in their series, *"Raising Antiracist Kids."*

Dr. Berry speaks on these topics and is actively involved in training leaders across the United States. www.brownicity.com

The Color of Compromise MasterLecture Series
Jemar Tisby

This study provides an in-depth diagnosis for a racially divided American church and suggests ways to foster a more equitable and inclusive environment among God's people.

Tisby is a PhD candidate in history at the University of Mississippi, focusing on race, religion, and social movements in the twentieth century. He is also cohost of the Pass the Mic podcast. He speaks at conferences nationwide and has written for *New York Times, The Atlantic,* and CNN.

www.masterlectures.zondervanacademic.com/the-color-of-compromise-jemar-tisby

*Rethinking Incarceration: Advocating for Justice that
Restores*
Dominique DuBois Gilliard

This study argues that God's justice is relational, and inher-
ently restorative. Examining the secular and church history
through which we have ultimately arrived at having more
people incarcerated than any country in the history of the
world, Gilliard illustrates how Christians have been complicit in constructing a justice system that is anything but
just. Ultimately, Gilliard points to practical steps forward to
advocate for our neighbors.

https://walkingtowardslove.com/series/rethinking-
incarceration/

Acknowledgments

To my wife, Dara: Tell me that story again, the one that has no ending. That will be the story of you and me.

To my kids, Max, Mary, Jack, and Benjamin: Choose Jesus and share His love with others. I love being your dad.

To Lily: Forever in Mommy and Daddy's heart. You are the first from our family to enjoy Jesus face to face. We cannot wait to meet you.

To my mother, Becky Docusen: You taught me how to pray when you did not know I was listening as a child. Thank you for believing in me and showing me the way to Jesus.

To my father, David Docusen, Sr. and Sheryl: Dad, you gave me your name and your passion for creativity, excellence, and hard work. Thank you both for your love and support.

To my father and mother by marriage, Darrell and Marvel Pope: You welcomed me into your family and into your hearts. Thank you for loving me and trusting me with your girl.

To my siblings, Leah (and your family), Brandon (and your family), Journey, and Tori (and your family): We are always together, no matter where life takes us. I love you.

To Linda and Mark Derringer: From my office in Orlando to holding this book in your hands, you have loved and believed in Dara and me. Thank you for your investment into our lives and in our call to share this message with the world. You and your family are loved.

To my family and friends, of whom you know your name: I have been blessed with the gift of family that is connected by far more than our blood, and friends who are as close to my heart as family. Thank you for your prayers and encouragement.

To my agent, Esther Fedorkevich, and the team at the Fedd Agency: Thank you for believing in me. You told me to patiently wait until the message was formed in my heart. This book is the fruit of those wise words.

To my editor, Tori Thacher: Your words and mine seamlessly blended together to shape the message of neighborliness. You are brilliant and courageous. Thank you.

To Mark and Lora Batterson: Thank you for creating new pathways for Dara and me to follow.

To Doug Witherup (and the Multiply Family of Churches): Our paths continue to cross at significant moments in our lives. Thank you for your example, generosity, and friendship.

To John and Susie James (and the entire Bethany Church family): You are dear friends that became family. We love and appreciate you and our NJ church family.

To our Access Church family in Lakeland, FL: Jason and Lis Burns (and family), Ryan and Julie Jordan (and family), thanks for believing in this message and for your constant friendship, encouragement, and generosity.

To everyone who found home at Center City Church: God's Word is a lamp to guide your feet and a light for your path. I pray that you wouldn't stray off left and right where there is darkness and confusion, but that you'd stay on the path that's lit by the light of God's Word. Amen. (Psalm 119:105)

To the faculty, administration, staff, and alumni of South-eastern University: The content of this book is marked by your influence. Thank you for your investment into my life.

To my Freedom Communities and West Charlotte family: Thank you for helping me see the beauty of God in our friendship, passion, and shared expression of faith.

About the Author

David Docusen has spent twenty years investing into communities as a pastor, speaker, teacher, advocate, and author. After pastoring in the local church for twenty years, David and his wife, Dara, launched Docusen Ministries. Through this organization, David invests into churches, nonprofits, and businesses across the world through speaking, teaching, and writing.

After completing his doctoral degree studying the cyclical patterns of generational poverty, he worked with a group of businesspeople as a founding board member of Freedom Communities—an organization that focuses on equitable access to education, employment, healthcare, and housing. He is on the Board of Trustees and an adjunct practical theology professor at Southeastern University, and he also serves as a member of the Executive Board of Relevant Magazine, helping shape vision and culture for the organization.

David and Dara live in Charlotte, North Carolina with their four kids: Max, Mary, Jack, and Ben.

Endnotes

OPENING PRAYER

1   Phyllis Tickle, *The Divine Hours: Prayers for Summertime* (New York: Image Books, 2006).

CHAPTER 1

2   Clint Smith, "The Danger of Silence," accessed June 1, 2020, https://www.ted.com/talks/clint_smith_the_danger_of_silence.

3   Nancy J. Duff, "The Second Great Commandment," *Journal for Preachers* 34, no. 4 (2011): 18.

CHAPTER 2

4   Lisa Rab, "Our Lowest Low," *Charlotte Magazine*, February 5, 2016, http://www.charlottemagazine.com/Charlotte-Magazine/February-2016/The-Conversation-Issue-50-Our-Lowest-Low.

5   Peter Moskowitz, *How to Kill a City: Gentrification, Inequality, and the Fight for the Neighborhood* (New York: Nation Books, 2017), Kindle.

6   Melissa De Witte, "Jackelyn Hwang's Research on Gentrification in Stanford News," August 28, 2019, https://sociology.stanford.edu/news/jackelyn-hwangs-research-gentrification-stanford-news.

7   Roslyn Arlin Mickelson, Stephen Samuel Smith, and Amy Hawn Nelson. *Yesterday, Today, and Tomorrow: School Desegregation and Resegregation in Charlotte.* 12.

8   Ibid., 12.

9   Ibram X. Kendi. *How To Be an Antiracist.* S.1: Vintage, 2020. 17.

10   Avidit Acharya, Matthew Blackwell, and Maya Sen, "Explaining Preferences from Behavior: A Cognitive Dissonance Approach," PDF file, 2018, http://stanford.edu/~avidit/preferences.pdf.

11   Personal conversation with Bob Goff.

CHAPTER 3

12   Phil Hissom originally posed this question to the Center City Church family during a seminar he was teaching called *Dignity Serves*. www.dignityserves.com

13   Kendi, Ibram X. *How To Be an Antiracist*. S.1: Vintage, 2020.

14   C. S. Lewis. *The Four Loves*. San Francisco: HarperOne, 2017.

CHAPTER 4

15   Mark Charles, and Soong-Chan Rah. *Unsettling Truths: The Ongoing, Dehumanizing Legacy of the Doctrine of Discovery*. Downers Grove, IL: IVP, an imprint of InterVarsity Press, 2019. 13.

16   Soong-Chan Rah. *Many Colors: Cultural Intelligence for a Changing Church*. Chicago: Moody Publishers, 2010. 117.

17   Tisby, Jemar. *Color of Compromise: The Truth About the American Church's Complicity in Racism*. S.1.: Zondervan, 2020.17.

18   Mark Charles, Twitter post, April 2016, 12:19 p.m. https://twitter.com/wirelesshogan/status/717401329803636737/photo/1

19   For a detailed overview of these topics, see Michelle Alexander's book *The New Jim Crow* and Mark Charles' and Soong-Chan Rah's book *Unsettling Truths*.

CHAPTER 5

20   *Trouble I've Seen: Changing the Way the Church Views Racism*. Harrisonburg, VA: Herald Press, 2016.

21   Timothy J. Keller. *Center Church: Doing Balanced, Gospel-centered Ministry in Your City* (Grand Rapids, MI: Zondervan, 2012), 154.

CHAPTER 6

22 Michelle Alexander. *The New Jim Crow: Mass Incarceration in the Age of Colorblindness*. New York: New Press, 2010. 1.

23 Ibid., 112.

24 Ibid., 6.

25 Dominique Dubois Gilliard. *Rethinking Incarceration: Advocating for Justice That Restores*. IVP Books, 2018. 26.

26 *Color of Compromise: The Truth About the American Church's Complicity in Racism*. S.l.: 2020.

27 The RSA. "Brené Brown on Empathy." YouTube.com, 2013, www.youtube.com/watch?v=1Evwgu369Jw.

28 Soong-Chan Rah. *Prophetic Lament: A Call for Justice in Troubled Times*. Downers Grove, PA: IVP Books, 2015. 21.

CHAPTER 7

29 "UrbanPromise Charlotte," UrbanPromise Charlotte, accessed June 1, 2020, https://www.urbanpromisecharlotte.org/.

30 Robert D. Putnam. *Our Kids: The American Dream in Crisis*. New York: Simon & Schuster, 2015. Kindle Location 3336.

31 Jacques Ellul. *Money & Power*. Eugene, Or.: Wipf & Stock, 2009. 101.

CHAPTER 8

32 *Toxic Charity: How Churches and Charities Hurt Those They Help (and How to Reverse It)*. New York: HarperOne, 2012.

CHAPTER 9

33 Ronald J. Sider. *Rich Christians in an Age of Hunger: Moving from Affluence to Generosity*. Nashville, TN: Thomas Nelson, 1997, 67.

34   Stevenson, Bryan. *Just Mercy: A Story of Justice and Redemption.* Melbourne: Scribe, 2020. 42.

35   Neil Cole. *Church 3.0: Upgrades for the Future of the Church.* San Francisco, CA: Jossey-Bass, 2010. 86.

36   "Quality, Affordable Healthcare," accessed June 8, 2020, http://www.lawndale.org/.

37   "Purpose Built Communities," accessed June 8, 2020, http://www.purposebuiltcommunities.org/.

38   "DC Dream Center," accessed June8, 2020, www.dcdreamcenter.org

39   "Christian Community Development Association," accessed June 8, 2020, http://www.ccda.org/.

40   "Doctor of Ministry," accessed June 8, 2020, https://www.seu.edu/academics/programs/doctor-of-ministry-2/.

CHAPTER 10

41   City Gospel Movements, "Visionary Women: Nicole Martin on Scripture Engagement," February 18, 2020, https://citygospelmovements.org/podcast/visionary-women-nicole-martin-on-scripture-engagement/.

42   "Lift Orlando," Lift Orlando, accessed June 1, 2020, http://www.liftorlando.org/.

43   Lift Orlando, "Collective Impact," November 22, 2016, video, https://www.youtube.com/watch?v=NUitsXupvj4.

44   Lift Orlando, "Place Based Initiatives," December 6, 2016, video, https://www.youtube.com/watch?v=mnpdXfrv8X8.

45   Lift Orlando, "Asset Based Community Development," December 6, 2016, video, https://www.youtube.com/watch?v=BlAIUEf-Dyzg.

46   John P. Kretzmann and John L. McKnight, *Building Communities from the Inside Out: A Path toward Finding and Mobilizing a Community's Assets* (Chicago: ACTA Publications, 1993), 6.

47   Phil Hissom, "Mission," July 4, 2019, http://www.polisinstitute.org/about.

48   Philip K. Hissom, "Thriving Cities: City Profile of Orlando" (Charlottesville, VA: University of Virginia Institute for Advanced Studies of Culture, 2017), http://polisinstitute.org/City-Profile-Orlando.pdf.

49   My doctoral dissertation is available for download at https://fire-scholars.seu.edu/dmin/5/.

50   Phil Hissom, "Best-In-Class Training," Polis Institute, June 18, 2019, http://www.dignityserves.com/.

51   Walter Brueggemann. *The Prophetic Imagination*. Philadelphia: Fortress Press, 1978. 3.

52   Mark Batterson. *Double Blessing: How to Get It, How to Give It*. Colorado Springs, CO: Multnomah Books, 2020. 193.

CHAPTER 11

53   Walter Brueggemann, *Isaiah 40-66* (Lexington, KY: Westminster John Knox, 1998), 186.

54   John Goldingay, *The Theology of the Book of Isaiah* (Downers Grove, IL: IVP Academic, 2014), 87.

55   James K. A. Smith, *You Are What You Love: the Spiritual Power of Habit*. Grand Rapids, MI: Brazos Press, a division of Baker Publishing Group, 2016. 13.

56   Joseph A. Fitzmyer, *The Gospel according to Luke: Introduction, Translation, and Notes* (Garden City, N.Y.: Doubleday, 1985), 1110.

57   Ronald Sider. *Rich Christians in an Age of Hunger*. 111.

58   Jacques Ellul. *Money and Power*. 84.

59   Ronald Sider, *Rich Christians in an Age of Hunger*. 68.

60   John Oswalt, *The Book of Isaiah, Chapters 40-66*, Location 9750, Kindle.

CHAPTER 12

61   Peter Moskowitz. *How to Kill a City*.

STUDY GUIDE

62   Mark Charles, "The Truth behind 'We the People' - the Three Most Misunderstood Words in US History," TED, accessed June 8, 2020, https://www.ted.com/talks/mark_charles_the_truth_behind_we_the_people_the_three_most_misunderstood_words_in_us_history/up-next.

63   Lucretia Berry and TEDx Talks, "Children Will Light up the World If We Don't Keep Them in the Dark," *YouTube* video, 13:43, 2017, https://www.youtube.com/watch?v=q0YDt64IWFU.